IN THE
SHADOWS
OF PARIS

ALSO BY ANNE SINCLAIR

My Grandfather's Gallery:
A Family Memoir of Art and War

~

IN FRENCH

Une année particulière
Deux ou trois choses que je sais d'eux
Caméra subjective
21, rue La Boétie
Chronique d'une France blessée
Passé composé

Kenneth Kales, Editor
Sandra Smith, Translator
Bonnie Thompson, Associate Editor
Rima Weinberg, Assistent Editor

Jacket design by Laura Klynstra
Book design by Jennifer Houle

Library of Congress Cataloging-in-Publication Data

Library of Congress Cataloging-in-Publication Data
Names: Sinclair, Anne, author. | Smith, Sandra, 1949–translator.
Title: In the shadows of Paris : the Nazi concentration camp that dimmed the city of light / Anne Sinclair ;
    Sandra Smith, translator.
Other titles: La Rafle des notables. English | Nazi concentration camp that dimmed the city of light Description: First edition. | San Diego, California : Kales Press, [2021] | Originally published as "La rafle des notables" by Éditions Grasset & Fasquelle, 2020. | Includes bibliographical references. | Summary: "'This story has haunted me since I was a child,' begins Anne Sinclair in a personal journey to find answers about her own life and about her grandfather's, Léonce Schwartz. What her tribute reveals is part memoir, part historical documentation of a lesser-known chapter of the Holocaust: the Nazis' mass arrest, in French the word for this is rafle, and there is no equivalent in English that captures the horror, on December 12, 1941, of prominent Jews—the doctors, professors, artists, and others at the upper levels of French society—who were then imprisoned just fifty miles from Paris in the Compiègne-Royallieu concentration camp. Those who did not perish there were taken by the infamous one-way trains to Auschwitz; except for the few to escape that fate. Léonce Schwartz was among them'—Provided by publisher.
Identifiers: LCCN 2021025764 (print) | LCCN 2021025765 (ebook) | ISBN 9781733395861 (print) | ISBN 9781733395878 (ebook)
Subjects: LCSH: Schwartz, Léonce. | Royallieu (Transit camp)—Biography. | Concentration camp inmates—France—Compiègne—Biography. | World War, 1939-1945—Prisoners and prisons, French. | Jews—France—Paris—Biography. | Holocaust, Jewish (1939-1945)—France. | Paris (France)—Biography.
Classification: LCC D805.5.R69 S56 2021 (print) | LCC D805.5.R69 (ebook) | DDC 940.53/18094436i—dc23
LC record available at https://lccn.loc.gov/2021025764
LC ebook record available at https://lccn.loc.gov/2021025765

First Edition
Printed in the United States of America

ISBN-13: 978-1-7333958-6-1 print edition
ISBN-13: 978-1-7333958-7-8 ebook edition
kalespress.com
San Diego, California

IN THE
SHADOWS
OF PARIS

The Nazi Concentration Camp That
Dimmed the City of Light

ANNE SINCLAIR

KALES✤PRESS

For my sons, David and Elie,
and for my grandchildren

I have dreamed so vividly
of you — I have so often
walked, so often spoken
so intensely loved your shadow
that nothing of you remains any longer
for me — except
to be the shadow between the
shadows
the shadow who will come
again and again into your life
drenched in sunlight

CONTENTS

PREFACE

This story has haunted me since I was a child. And yet, while family history seems more interesting as people get older, my own story interested me only from a distance, at least at first, because for a long time, as a journalist, I found what was happening in the present more compelling than stories about the past. Nevertheless, this particular moment in time continued to obsess me. Was it because of the romantic aspect that I couldn't explain, the questions I didn't ask, the details I never pursued?

I was raised with the belief that children didn't ask questions of adults, and since we weren't entrusted with any secrets, it seemed improper to pry. Besides, those secrets were a burden on us. Listening to stories told by the older members of my family, stories we couldn't care less about and that we couldn't fully understand, embarrassed us and encroached on our playtime. Despite all that, later on I could have tried to find out more. Why didn't I, and why didn't my father tell me anything, even though from a rather young age I'd loved it when he read to me from his war journal, leaving out the pages that were inappropriate for an adolescent?

But when I finally did try, I quickly learned the basic facts of the epic journey of my maternal family, the Rosenbergs: their escape from France on June 16 and 17, 1940; the looting of everything they'd owned; and their arrival in America. Moreover, this story moved me to give an account of those events,[2] one that merged art, the war, the great tragic history of that time, our family's story, and the ironies of fate, and resulted in the publication of *My Grandfather's Gallery: A Family Memoir of Art and War*.

In that book I also touched on research into the other story, the one about my paternal family, without going deeper at the time. But it kept calling out to my heart because, as is most often true, when the witnesses disappear, when there is no one left to confirm or tell the story, it becomes a matter of urgency, for the fragments of memory that reach us will disappear after us, unless they reach others as well.

When I began my more fervent research into Léonce Schwartz, my father's father, I hoped to unearth some leads about his arrest—which I thought had been made by French police sympathizing with the German occupiers— and about his incarceration, which I was sure had been at Drancy.[3] I also believed I'd be able to clarify one of our family's legends: my grandfather's fantastical escape from a concentration camp, thanks to my grandmother's courage.

Disguised as a nurse, she'd stolen a Red Cross ambulance, sneaked into the camp, and hid him in the back, narrowly preventing his deportation. I assumed I would find documents and letters, and that from these things I could also learn about their hiding place during the war years that followed. And then, I thought without a trace of modesty, I would feed on my research and its puzzles to produce a literary narrative on the coattails of Patrick Modiano's *Dora Bruder*.

After several months of investigating, though, and resigned to finding virtually no documents in my family's possession, I realized that the rare discoveries I'd made hardly confirmed what I had believed. In fact, quite to the contrary. The arrest had been made by the Nazi Wehrmacht, not by the men under the French collaborators René Bousquet and Jean Leguay. And he had been detained not at Drancy but at the transit and internment camp Frontstalag 122, at Royallieu-Compiègne, which was lesser known. Also, there had been no romantic escape past the barbed wire; my grandmother's adventure to get my grandfather out of the Nazis' claws was true, but it was from the bed of the Val-de-Grâce hospital, not from the barracks of the camp.

So I went to Compiègne and was struck once again by how much these now-sanitized places have lost their emotional impact. I had already felt that when I'd visited Auschwitz-Birkenau: innumerable books had had an emotive power over me that was a hundred times stronger than what I felt once I was actually seeing the fragile wood of the birch trees, the vast, snow-covered expanses of land crossed by railroad tracks, the piles of stones, the vestiges of the gas chambers that I could only imagine. I had cried over stories of people who had survived, from Primo Levi to Imre Kertész and Marceline Loridan-Ivens, but at Auschwitz itself I was not overwhelmed by emotion as I had expected to be.

Compiègne did not make me feel anything either, except for my astonishment at its incredible proximity to Paris, via the highway that runs along the edge of the camp, today called the Avenue des Martyrs de la Liberté; in the past, it had simply been referred to as the road from Paris to Saint-Quentin. It made me think of the very busy Avenida del Libertador, which crosses Buenos Aires and runs along the edge of the barbed wire of the Escuela Superior de Mecánica de la Armada (ESMA), originally a naval engineering school, until, at the beginning of the 1980s, thousands of victims of Jorge Rafael Videla's generals were tortured there, right in the middle of the city. When I visited that site, which holds such sad memories for Argentinians, I remember saying to myself, *It's unthinkable that they could hide a place of torture for such a long time right beside an enormous highway.*

And so I read. All the monographs written about the Nazi camp at Royallieu-Compiègne, the journals of people who had been prisoners there and who had survived, as well as notes people had written on the trains, the trains taking them to their deaths, throwing their pieces of paper out onto the railroad tracks. Of course, I consulted the work of Serge Klarsfeld, who for fifteen or twenty years had undertaken the formidable task of publishing those narratives, making it possible for their stories, very often devastating ones, to see the light of day.

In the narratives written by historians, on the other hand, I did not find many details about the *"rafle* of prominent Jews,"[4] which happened after the first *rafles* of May and August 1941, and before the one called the "Vél' d'Hiv" of July 1942, which has since become known as an important event in World War II history.[5]

Though lesser known, this *rafle* of prominent Jews on December 12, 1941, is also important: it targeted 743 French Jews for imprisonment at Royallieu-Compiègne, people from an influential upper-middle-class population who had been living in France for a long time. Three hundred foreign Jews, men who were far less socially advantaged, were also transferred there from the camp at Drancy, to allow the authorities of the Occupation to reach Berlin's goal of a total of at least one thousand Frontstalag 122 Jewish prisoners.

These two groups of people, whose lives had not intersected up to that point, thus found themselves together at this concentration camp: highly regarded French Jews who were very assimilated and foreign Jews who had been subject to harassment, hatred, and pogroms for a very long time. They had highly divergent approaches to Judaism and different understandings of the reasons for their arrests. Nevertheless, in just a few weeks, their torturers would transform all of them into the same mass of suffering humanity.

The ultimate aim of this *rafle* was, of course, deportation to death camps. To German officials like Otto Abetz, the German ambassador to France, this was perfectly compatible with the global Nazi plan. Adolf Hitler had met with Ambassador Abetz on August 3, 1940, before the emissary returned to his post in Paris, and told him of his "plan to rid Europe of all its Jews."[6]

In fact, it was from the camp at Royallieu-Compiègne that an initial group of Jews was deported out of France. The majority of the prisoners there were sent to Auschwitz[7] on March 27, 1942, and most of them perished in its gas chambers over the following days. The others, despite first being transferred from Royallieu-Compiègne to

Drancy (some of them having originally come from Drancy), still ended up taking the same route to the same death camp. Some of them were lucky enough to survive, to go home, or be freed, most often because of age or serious medical issues. That was the case for my grandfather, Léonce Schwartz, of whom I found some mention here and there in my research. Transferred to the Val-de-Grâce hospital, he miraculously escaped being sent to Auschwitz. But he died from the physical abuse inflicted upon him by the Germans, shortly following their surrender in May 1945. He had the privilege of dying in his own bed, a few weeks after the return of his beloved son, Robert, my father, from the Middle East; he had been sent there after enlisting with the Free French Forces, on the side of the Allies.

So this was very little information with which to write a family history. And writing a novel was out of the question, because I would have felt as if I were betraying the painful story of the few who had survived.

Nevertheless, I want people to know about this *rafle*, especially people who are not necessarily specialists in this period. I understand that it may not be of interest to those weary of such accounts, those whose attention has been dulled by the thousands of stories about the Shoah. Even so, I would simply like to pay homage to the men I did not know who suffered alongside my grandfather during their three months together, and to their loved ones—and perhaps, in this way, to lessen my guilt over not having attempted to unravel the threads of this story sooner.

I would also add that this terribly overwhelming chapter in twentieth-century history obsesses me, and the more time passes, the more it all seems obscure.

Faced with the rebirth of anti-Semitism and the extremism and populism now developing in Europe, the United States, and around the world, in ways that were unimaginable in my youth, I have become more and more haunted by the years of the Occupation.

Worse still is the dark hole of the Shoah, which remains unfathomable, impermeable to reason. Attempting to somewhat bring back to life those who died in the Holocaust has become a calling of mine. I hope that by writing this research-based account and reconstruction of events, I can root out my torment—the shadowy inhabitant of my own memory—over my own family history, and root out the burden that has become a collective memory.

Little by little, the tragedy of my grandfather's experience, which was the original object of my research, has been overtaken by the urgency of sharing with a greater number of people what he lived through, as well as what a thousand other Frenchmen lived through, too; this book is an attempt to lift out of the shadows facts that have mainly been known only to specialists in Holocaust studies. These people's narratives are poignant. References to them in these pages are a memorial to their victimization at the hands of the Nazis during a zealous persecution. This is why I want to tell the story of this *rafle* and this camp, so that people know what happened in France more than eighty years ago, a mere hour's drive from Paris.

The *rafle* of prominent Jews began on the night of December 12, 1941. Accounts of the *rafles* of that period all begin the same way, with more or less identical details, and they began the same way for the thousands of others who were arrested in occupied France, as well as for the millions of others in Nazi-controlled Europe: a doorbell rings, shattering the silence of the night. For my grandparents, it was at No. 46 on the affluent Rue de Tocqueville in Paris, in the Seventeenth Arrondissement.

IN THE
SHADOWS
OF PARIS

I

THE ARREST

I t is between five-thirty and seven on Friday morning when Léonce and Marguerite Schwartz, my paternal grandparents, are pulled from their bed.

I can picture them, the Sunday before, at the tennis club where they often went, neglecting to take precautions, playing bridge with their friends, watching the happy young people carrying tennis rackets come and go, heroes of a small social circle oblivious to the dangers others faced.

They often used the surname Sabatier, but at the club, everyone knew them by Schwartz. This despite the statute regarding Jews, the one decreed by the Vichy government the previous October and extended in June, and especially despite the census the Germans had conducted

in October 1940 and the later one known as the "verifica-
tion," carried out between October and November 1941;
despite the *rafle* of May aimed at foreign Jews, then the
one in August, when, for the first time, Frenchmen were
arrested, including some forty Jewish lawyers. Despite all
this, they were determined not to live in fear of what they
could not control. Though my grandfather had temporarily closed his wholesale lace business on the Rue d'Abou-
kir to avoid any risk of Aryanization,[8] life went on—albeit
with increasing oppression.

Like many of their friends, they had not wanted to flee
to the Free Zone[9] or abroad. Nor did they wish to hide or
move. Was this irresponsible? After all, the concierge had
always greeted them with a loud "Hello, Monsieur and
Madame Schwartz," just as she greeted Louis and Mariette
Engelmann, the tenants on the floor above. And besides,
with full disbelief of the warnings, they reassured themselves that they'd be safe, confident that there was no
reason they'd arrest Léonce. Just as did Jean-Jacques
Bernard, the son of Tristan Bernard,[10] described in his
very beautiful book *The Camp of Slow Death:* "I didn't
really believe it. There was nothing they could accuse
me of."[11] Which says a great deal about the blindness

of the Jews then in the face of the Nazis' desire to eliminate them.

My grandmother was happy to know that their daughter, my aunt Denise, was in Cannes, in the Free Zone, with her children, waiting to go to Switzerland to join her husband. My father, Robert, was even farther away, having left for America and, according to my grandparents, "God only knows where afterward." He had managed to get word to them six months before to say that he was all right. But he had said nothing about his plans, so they had no idea that he was in the Middle East, fighting with the Free French Forces, and had nearly died of dysentery in a hospital in Damascus.

Fortunately, their group of friends did not break up during this fractious time, in part because all of them had agreed never to discuss politics when they were together. Some of their friends liked the nationalist hero Maréchal Philippe Pétain and thought he was doing everything possible to improve the fate of France, while some of their other friends were disgusted by Pétain's regime and, my grandparents suspected, listened to the Free French station Radio London at their children's homes. And then there were some who said nothing; only when they found themselves alone with their families did they allow their sighs and worries to be heard: What was going to happen to this country, to this France, to themselves?

A few weeks earlier, on September 5, 1941, an exhibition had opened at the Palais Berlitz titled *Le Juif et la France* (The Jew and France), under the aegis of the Institute for the Study of the Jewish Question, a French office of Nazi propaganda run by the Gestapo. As they passed the building, on the Boulevard des Italiens, my grandparents trembled, seeing the repugnant poster of a man with bulging eyes clutching a globe of the world in his clawlike hands. Many people attended the show, eager to know, as the publicity promised, "How to distinguish a Jew from a Frenchman." The ironic part of this is that the exhibition had been conceived at 21 Rue La Boétie, in the office of the Institute for the Study of the Jewish Question, located in the building of the "Jew Rosenberg,"[12] who would become, after the war, father-in-law to my grandparents' son, my father, Robert.

From the research, we can reconstruct the arrests by the descriptions of those who lived through them, including the Schwartz side of my own family, described them. A finger rings the bell, impatiently. Startled, the residents go to open the door at that early hour, having read accounts of the police arriving at dawn in Stalin's Soviet Union to arrest his opponents, and of Nazis doing the same in Germany, ever since 1933, to grab enemies of the regime—in particular, the Jews.

I wanted to go see 46 Rue de Tocqueville, where my grandparents had lived. It is located on a very peaceful part of the street, a short walk from the Parc Monceau. In the widest part of the road, lined with linden trees, cars can park on a center island. The trees are young. They were not here back then. The building is typical of the vast renovations of Paris begun in 1853, during a period known as the Haussmann era,[13] though today it is protected by two locks that require digital codes for entry. I sneak in when a young employee of Chronopost[14] comes out, and stand for a moment between the door that leads to the street and another door, a glass one, which is also closed. *I don't know what I was expecting by coming here. I don't even know what floor they lived on.* I have no memory of the building either, although I do know I visited my grandmother there—I was just five years old—to watch

the coronation of the queen of England in 1953; my grandmother was the only one in our family who owned a
television then.

And so I stand for several long minutes in the entrance-
way, uncertain about whether I am dreaming, or having a
nightmare, or if I'm taking refuge from the pouring rain
on this October day when the skies are barely clearer than
on that early morning of December 12, 1941 . . .

I picture them, the four men at the door. Two policemen
wearing capes and caps, and behind them, in uniform, two
soldiers of the Wehrmacht, then under the authority of the
German military commander in France, General Otto von
Stülpnagel. This is the accepted procedure for *rafles*: the
French police followed by two from the Feldgendarmerie,[15]
and sometimes by Gestapo agents, too.

"We're looking for Monsieur Léonce Schwartz." The
exchanges are the same in all the buildings visited at
dawn. "We would like you to come with us so we can ask
you a few questions," the Frenchmen say, while the
Germans remain silent. The theater's scenery is well
known, the dialogue easy to imagine. "Shall we give you

time to pack a small suitcase? It will only take forty-eight hours—"

"You have fifteen minutes," interrupts one of the Germans, in correct French but with a strong accent. His tone of voice conveys his belief in the superiority of the occupying forces; the two Frenchmen are obviously here only to set the stage. They hand my grandfather a list of what he is allowed to take with him: two blankets, some clothing, enough food for two days, a maximum of 3oo francs, no pen or paper.

Léonce, like all the others arrested that morning, does not ask why they've come at daybreak. He goes into the bedroom with my grandmother. It is cold, still dark outside. They grab a small suitcase. Marguerite quickly throws in a warm suit, some woolens, two blankets, while Léonce prepares his toiletries and, most importantly, his asthma medicine. He does not even think of fleeing. Anyway, how could he get out with the two Germans standing in the kitchen, blocking the service entrance?

They do not speak to each other. Acting quickly, Léonce has no idea what to say to his wife to reassure her. Besides, there is nothing reassuring about this. A quick kiss. The same idiotic words probably said by everyone taken that morning: "I'll try to get in touch as soon as I can." I can picture the indescribable smile on the face of the German who had spoken. The French police raise their caps to salute Marguerite and usher Léonce out; the Germans follow behind. The door of the building slams shut.

My grandmother stands frozen to the spot. There is noise in the hallway. Apparently, Louis Engelmann, who lives on the floor above, was also taken away. She dares not open the door to look. She rushes to the telephone and calls their closest Jewish friends. "They've just arrested Léonce. It's a *rafle*, don't stay at home," she whispers.

The filthy war has entered my grandparents' house. It is December 12, 1941, and they do not know that the "*rafle* of prominent Jews*" is just beginning.

Léonce gets into a car, which takes him to the town hall of the Seventeenth Arrondissement, on the Rue des Batignolles. Not a word is exchanged with the men accompanying him. He is pushed into a large room, already half full, and onto one of the benches of the expansive chamber, probably the place where marriages are performed. There are only men here, of all ages, visibly pulled from their beds, wearing hats and coats, with small suitcases at their feet. He recognizes Louis Engelmann, his upstairs neighbor, already sitting two rows in front of him; they nod to each other.

My grandfather would learn afterward that Louis was arrested at the bedside of his dying mother, then taken to 46 Rue de Tocqueville to get his things.[16] He remained there for several hours, without daring to speak, watched by the *Feldgendarmes* and the police of the Sipo-SD,[17] their French counterparts having disappeared.

Ideas keep churning through Léonce's mind, surely trivial and common ones: *I forgot to bring my shaving soap. . . . I should have had a glass of water. . . . When will I have the chance to drink something? . . . Margot must be worried sick. . . . How did we not realize that the census the Germans ordered in October 1940 and extended a month ago was a sign? It was madness not to have at least fled to the Free Zone! . . . And to think that I haven't been to synagogue since Robert's bar mitzvah and Denise's wedding! . . . But I'm French, I was born in Paris, I fought in the war of 1914. There must be some mistake . . .*

Even though the rumor that it's coming has been circulating for some time, the edict demanding that Jews wear a yellow star to identify themselves has not yet become law in France, unlike in the other countries occupied by the Reich. It will be put into effect in May 1942, when Reinhard Heydrich, who is responsible for the Jewish Question in Europe, travels to France.

"Pointless to try to talk," Louis Engelmann, his neighbor, quickly whispers to Léonce; another man who tries to is threatened and told to keep quiet by the soldiers standing watch.

Day breaks on this gray December day, cold and somber. The hours pass by, interrupted only by the arrival of others sharing the same misfortune. At the end of the morning, they hear a noise from outside; soon after, these men arrested at dawn are led out, one by one. Buses are waiting for them in front of the town hall, where a few curious people watch in silence. Then begins the long trek through Paris. Once they arrive at the École Militaire, other soldiers, who appear to be expecting them, get Léonce and the rest of the men out of the bus, hitting them with the butts of their rifles to move them along. The men's first encounter with shouting and brutality.

They enter a large hall that is dark and full of sand, the "riding arena of Commandant L. Bossut," as the young engineer Georges Kohn, also arrested in that day's *rafle*, will write.[18] The structure had been the riding school of the École Supérieure de Guerre (the Superior School of War). It is a long, narrow space, fifty meters long and ten meters wide. At the end is a small platform where the Germans have just set up a machine gun, which they move from side to side; this threat amuses the soldiers a great deal, as well as the German nurses who have joined them, as Georges Kohn will note.[19]

I go to see that riding arena behind Les Invalides. Today there is a training session for the soldiers. I have to sneak in because visitors are not allowed.

I push open a door that is ajar and encounter a young man. I ask him if he might show me where I can find the commemorative plaque that explains that 743 prominent Frenchmen were held here before being sent to Royallieu-Compiègne. I know it was put here in 1999 by the Sons and Daughters of Jewish Deportees from France (FFDJF) to honor the memory of the people arrested on December 12, 1941.

"A plaque? What plaque? I've been here for ten years and I've never seen one." He calls a colleague over, the building manager. "How long have you been here?"

"Nineteen years."

"And have you ever seen a plaque? This lady's looking for it."

A doubtful frown.

They take me all around the building. It is not there. And I discover it only when I leave: outside, on the wall that overlooks the esplanade of the École Militaire, exactly where it should be, accessible to the public, not just to the soldiers. The guards have never noticed it, which puts into perspective memorial inscriptions: so many are thought to be important but go unseen by the people who live or work near them.[20]

The gray day has yet to lift. The arena endlessly fills up: the Nazis have taken the crème de la crème of Jews from every corner of Paris. Some prisoners greet each other, hug, reassured to see a friendly face amid their misfortune. Most of the men, mainly in their fifties, wear the elegant, tailored clothing of people who want for nothing. Surely my grandfather recognizes some friends, or people from his neighborhood.

The new arrivals cause dust to fill the air. It mixes with the horse dung from the arena, making it unbreathable. Throats begin to hurt, but still not a single drop of water is offered. The men stand against the wall. Some of them attempt to sit down and are ordered to get up, always in the same menacing tone. As the hours go by, the detainees' natural needs become urgent. There is nowhere to be alone, so it is in a corner, in the sawdust, that the men, one by one, go to urinate, in front of the others, the beginning of the humiliating violations of decency against these well-positioned, upper-middle-class men, this one a violation that soon will no longer embarrass them at all.

Theodor Dannecker makes his entrance. The maniacal *SS-Hauptsturmführer* is the equivalent of a captain in the SS, the Schutzstaffel.[21] The prisoners quickly learn to know and fear him. Tall and elegant, he is here to supervise the mission, although it is officially led by the Militärbefehlshaber[22] and not the SS. He shouts orders in German, which most of the prisoners cannot understand.

Those who do catch a few words as he unleashes a torrent of abuse and threats: "Filthy pigs, sons of bitches, you'll see what's going to happen to you."[23]

The day goes by, interminably; the men pace up and down, talk to one another, wonder why they've been arrested.

It has often been surmised that this *rafle* of December 12 took place because of Pearl Harbor, immediately after which the United States entered the war. In fact, after reading the documents collected by Georges Wellers,[24] a prominent French biochemist and historian specializing in Nazism, who was himself arrested that day in the *rafle* and who would be deported to Auschwitz but would survive, I have come to understand that the mission was conceived before then. The arrest order came on December 5, 1941, two days before Pearl Harbor. Further, there had been a series of French anti-German attacks in October and November of that year. The Resistance fighters captured, especially the famous ones at Châteaubriant, would be executed; and these attacks served as a pretext for the occupiers' answer to the "Jewish Question."[25]

General Carl-Heinrich von Stülpnagel, however, was hesitant about the policy of reprisals desired by Adolf Hitler because, after each anti-German attack, they led to more Germans being taken as hostages and shot. This policy seemed counterproductive to him. He preferred a targeted and "externalized" form of repression—that is to say, the deportation of Jewish and Communist political enemies. This approach is emphasized by Philippe Bernard, a journalist at *Le Monde* and the nephew of my grandparents' neighbors Louis and Mariette Engelmann. In his introduction to their book, he highlights how such a systematic policy contradicts the traditional narrative that claims French Jews were targeted only after November 1942, following the Allies' landing in North Africa and the Germans' occupation of the Southern Zone (formerly called the Free Zone). More importantly, Philippe counters the almost sadistic revisionist thesis detailed by Vichy after the liberation that the government of Maréchal Pétain had served as a shield to the French Jews. And yet the absurdity is still taken up by today's polemicists, despite it being continually disproven by every historian.

Moreover, from the month of August 1941 onward, the Nazis, by arresting French citizens, had tested Vichy's feeble ability to react. As for the *rafle* on December 12, it was significant to the Germans as evidence that any distinction between French Jews and other Jews was completely worthless. Adolf Hitler's anti-Semitism was based on a racial concept of Judaism, so even being a citizen of the French Republic would not protect a Jew. I would add that the Nazis' propaganda had led the French to believe that Jews were the enemies of France—for example, through the exhibition *The Jew and France;* and in the end, arresting those of every class allowed them to point the finger at the role of powerful, wealthy Jews in anti-German activities and the war and, therefore, to claim that Jews were the cause of all that had befallen the French.

The Canadian historian Michael Marrus and the American political scientist Robert Paxton are the authors of numerous books and articles about Vichy; their works on this subject preceded many by their French counterparts, especially those on the anti-Jewish policies of the marshal of France, Philippe Pétain; the French collaborator Pierre Laval; and the French admiral François Darlan. Doctors Marrus and Paxton were also the first historians to insist that the French authorities brought crucial aid to the Germans, in particular through promulgating laws governing the status of Jews in October 1940 and June 1941 — laws that were designed to demonstrate France's eagerness to collaborate on anti-Jewish policies.

Within the Jewish division of the prefecture of police set up after the Germans ordered a census of Jews on June 2, 1941, there was also a "Jewish dossier" administered by André Tulard, the head of the bureau at the time; he became the assistant director of the prefecture of police in the spring of 1942, thereby also taking on responsibility for foreigners. This dossier identified the 150,000 Jews listed in the census in the Département de la Seine, in alphabetical order, by street, profession, and nationality; it was a model of efficiency and kept up-to-date. Doctors Marrus and Paxton point out that "its development surpassed the letter of the German laws, thanks to its own zealous administrative action"[26] and that it provided a precise guide to the authorities of the Occupation for the arrests of December 1941 and a rehearsal for the *rafles* that followed.

René Blum, the director of the Ballets de Monte-Carlo and a brother of Léon Blum, the first Jewish prime minister of France, was among the 743 French Jews considered to be "prominent"—in German, the *einflussreiche Juden,* "influential Jews."[27] These were the men arrested and gathered in the December 12 *rafle*. As was Roger Masse, a graduate of the prestigious École Polytechnique and a former colonel in the French army; his brother, Pierre Masse, an eminent legal scholar, a senator, and a former member of French prime minister Georges Clemenceau's government, had been in custody since the beginning of August 1941 and would join him the next day at the "Bossut arena." Jacques Debré, an engineer and a brother of the famous doctor Robert Debré, was also held in the arena, along with Maître André Ullmo, the famous lawyer. As was Robert Dreyfus, an adviser to the high-level Court of Cassation; Édouard Laemlé, the president of the Court of Appeals of Paris; Jean-Jacques Bernard; and Maurice Goudeket, the husband of the famous French author Colette. The uniqueness of this *rafle,* in which thirteen of the men arrested were graduates of the prestigious École Polytechnique and fifty-five were recipients of France's highest order of merit, the Legion of Honor, was that it brought together a socially interwoven population, especially representative of the professional classes, as well as notable businessmen, including my grandfather.

Léonce was not an intellectual. He was a small business owner. He sold lace to wholesalers, lace he had commissioned in the Belgian town of Bruges. He came from a family that had arrived from Italy after the tenth century and settled in Mainz, Germany, then in Alsace, France, and whose ancestors were most likely German, just as was the case for the majority of the Jews of the region.

In the fourteenth century, the bubonic plague—the Black Death—would sow more seeds for the beginning of pogroms, persecutions, and burnings at the stake when Jews were accused of practicing ritualistic crimes against children and poisoning the water. Many were forced out of France's large cities, like Colmar and Strasbourg, leading them to work as hawkers, tanners, and cattle merchants, settling in small communities, melting into the background. This changed with the French Revolution, which, beginning in 1789, opened the way, in September 1791, for French Jews to be given citizenship.[28]

The first Schwartz I found in the records, Scheye Schwartz, was born in northeastern France around the year 1600 in the village of Westhoffen, which remained the birthplace of Schwartz families for many decades. The village's cemetery, its tombstones vandalized with swastikas in December 2019, bears witness to the long presence of many Jewish families, including the ancestors of Michel Debré, the "father" of the present-day Constitution of France, and those of Léon Blum, the three-time prime minister of France. In a very well-documented article in *Le Nouvel Observateur,* Claude Weill describes how in "a squat village of 1,591 souls and only one Jew, nestled off the main road that leads from Strasburg to Saverne," there still stands a beautiful, abandoned synagogue, as well as one of the oldest Jewish cemeteries in the region.[29]

My grandfather was born in Paris on April 30, 1878, the son of Isaïe Schwartz, who was then forty-four years old. Isaïe's father had been born in Strasbourg and was, therefore, one of the first to be emancipated from life in Westhoffen; he was a professor of music and a composer whose pieces were played, or so it is said, in the synagogue of Strasbourg.

Léonce was a handsome man. I have only two yellowing photos of him, apparently taken in the 1930s, which I found in my father's desk. In one he is wearing a three-piece suit, with a gold ring in the shape of a snake on the little finger of his right hand; the snake's eye is a tiny sapphire. My father always wore that ring—he never took it off—and after he died, in 1980, I wore it as I would have worn a signet ring, a symbol of a remarkable heritage. In 1941, my grandfather, aged sixty-three, was already part of well-off Jewish society in Paris; he ran his own business, lived comfortably, and played bridge with his friends. This was enough to make him a target on that perilous morning of December 12, 1941, when he got caught up in a terrifying medieval detour, right in the middle of the twentieth century.

The day is never-ending, broken up only by the new arrivals. At around seven p.m., the guards stand the prisoners in twos before shouting soldiers push them out of the arena, beating them with the butts of their rifles and shoving them with sharp bayonets, herding them into buses to be driven through Paris. The city is deserted, for the curfew was set at six p.m. after the anti-German attacks. My grandfather and the others, guarded by a soldier at the front of the bus, close to the driver, and two or three others on the open platform in the rear standing-room area, watch Paris pass by, wondering when they might once again be able to enjoy her as free men. The shuttling of more than seven hundred prisoners takes a long time, with only four buses allocated for the journey back and forth.

The prisoners arrive at the Gare du Nord, where their numbers will increase. The Gestapo expects to make one thousand arrests that day, and they have already added to their daily quota by arresting some forty Jews at random on the streets of Paris; these men arrive with no luggage, with only what they had on their backs at the moment they were taken. But since the *rafle* itself has not met the numerical goal, the Germans add three hundred other Jews, foreigners for the most part, who have been interned at Drancy since their arrests months before in the May and August *rafles*. They are obvious by their dirty cloth-ing, thin bodies, and pale faces, their appearance in sharp contrast to that of the "prominent Jews," even with their refined attire covered in sand from the riding arena. Soon there will be no difference between them, except in the perceptions of their Jewish identity.

As they're about to be crowded into train cars, their worries mount, a main one being *Will we be leaving France?* At the moment, they are suffering most from the lack of water. One of them, spotting a *Feldgendarme*, takes a chance and asks, "Water, please?" but his companions anxiously whisper to him to correct himself: *"Bitte, bitte."* The man, in German this time, asks, *"Wasser, bitte?"* but the soldier neither hears nor understands him.

They are now in a dark third-class railway carriage, piled in, their belongings on their knees. But at least they can sit down. More delays, more waiting. Some of them even complain, like travelers frustrated by late departures.

When the train finally starts to move, it is nearly eleven p.m. It does not move fast, but even so, in the dark neither my grandfather nor the other men can read the names of the stations they pass. A little while later, the train suddenly stops; the prisoners can make out the name of the station from a faintly lit sign: COMPIÈGNE. Léonce, like the others, is relieved to see that they are not very far from Paris.

There is no platform. They get off the train as best they can and step onto the rocky ground, holding their suitcases. Then more pushing and shoving, more impatient orders and blows with rifle butts and kicks that strike at random. They wait, in the cold rain that is beginning to fall, and in the mud. Two by two, they leave the station, stumbling at the end of this exhausting day. Most of them are ground down with fatigue, distressed and humiliated after having been transported like animals in the dark. But this is only the beginning.

The walk is trying. The men bump into each other, their suitcases hitting neighboring legs. They walk for four or five kilometers, passing through the silent town. The weakest men have their suitcases taken from them by force and given to the stronger or younger ones. The stragglers are constantly beaten, amid endless shouting and dogs barking in the hellish dark—those who live in Compiègne will remember the noise of that night for a long time to come. The men finally arrive at a large locked gate with wide bars, into the sudden glare of blinding spotlights aimed down on them from watchtowers. The gates open to allow the 1,037 prisoners inside. Including my grandfather.

They are each assigned a number, then pushed in groups of about thirty into large, rectangular buildings. Barracks with beds? No: there are only thin straw pallets on the ground. The prisoners throw themselves onto the first mats they see, dropping heavily down, without taking off their coats in the already very cold night. It is past two in the morning, nearly twenty-four hours since their arrests. It is December 13, 1941. The gates of Frontstalag 122 can be locked again. The expected cargo has arrived.

2

THE JEWISH CAMP

Awakened and abruptly brought back to consciousness after a few hours of restless sleep, they rush to the latrines, which they will soon learn to avoid as much as possible. The piercing cold and the gnawing hunger are their reliable companions.

My grandfather bundles up in his two blankets, but this is not the case for everyone, especially the men arrested the night before on the street, who could not bring any luggage. One detail, however, reassures those trying to grasp at even the slightest of hopes to fight their fears: *The Germans won't send us to the East if we don't have any warm clothes. So this is just being staged to terrify us, or at most a temporary situation.* Their naïveté slows them from questioning whether the Nazis possess any humanity at all.

By December 1941, Royallieu-Compiègne had become the third concentration camp opened in France, after the Natzweiler-Struthof camp in Alsace, opened in May of that year, and Drancy, the largest camp in France, opened three months later, in August. As the war continued, Drancy became the transit point for nine out of ten French Jews deported to Auschwitz, Buchenwald, and other death camps.

The location known as Royallieu is ancient. In the twelfth century, Queen Adelaide, the widow of the Capetian king Louis VI—also known by the nickname "le Gros," "the Fat"[30]—had a royal estate built here. This accounts for the name Royal-Lieu, or "Royal Place";[31] kings and queens of France spent summers at the estate until its destruction by the English in 1430. Barracks were built here in 1913, in the lead-up to War World I. The question remains as to whether the Germans set up a concentration camp here as a historical symbol, to scoff at their humiliating capitulation in the armistice of 1918, signed in a train car at Rethondes, in the Compiègne municipality. Two decades later, those same barracks were transformed into a military hospital[32] during the "Phony War."[33] In June 1940, the Germans placed French and British prisoners of war there, in what they called Frontstalag 122, before using those barracks to house civilians like my grandfather.

The concentration camp is a large quadrangle of thirty-nine acres, surrounded by walls and bordered on the east by the road that leads to Paris. I went there for the first time in 2018, while researching this book, as if I were going on my first pilgrimage. I returned at the beginning of October 2019, and by this point in my research, I was filled with the stories told by some of its prisoners.

All that remains are three large barracks and a garden, where memorial headstones are scattered about. This diminished space, on a human scale, does little to help a visitor envision the tragedies that took place here. I walked around the rectangular buildings, with their brick walls and tiled roofs that cleverly retrace the history of Frontstalag 122, from the train cars of Rethondes to the final deportations before the liberation; I tried to follow the traces left by those "prominent" Jewish men from 1941 and 1942, and by the poems of Robert Desnos, the French Resistance fighter who was sent to this camp.[34]

The barracks' walls are bare, the multiple layers of paint having been scraped away in an effort to try to find any messages from the unfortunate souls who were interned there. From the outside, the grounds look more like abandoned buildings than a concentration camp, and they have become the site of an extremely well-designed memorial museum established by the Compiègne Town Hall.

The story of this place is told less often than that of Drancy, considered of greater importance due to its size and its reputation as the antechamber of Auschwitz.[35] Nevertheless, for most of the Jewish prisoners sent to Royallieu-Compiègne, the destination would become their final stop before the death camps in Poland. It was also the point from which, throughout the Occupation, convoys known as "clampdown deportations" would leave, carrying the Jewish or French Resistance sympathizers arrested in reprisal for anti-German attacks.

There were four camps within three main areas at Frontstalag 122 in 1941, some of them housing civilian prisoners.[36] Camp A, also known as the "French Camp," was the one closest to the entrance gate, and held the political prisoners: three thousand men, mostly French Communists.

The shacks of Camp B, the "American Camp," newly emerged after the United States entered the war, shortly before the *rafle* we are describing began.

At the back, well away from the others, was a third camp, Camp C, standing perpendicular to Camp A, set apart by a double row of barbed wire. Prisoners risked their lives if they got too close to it, certain to be mowed down by machine-gun fire from the watchtowers. Those in this segregated area, called the "Jewish Camp," were subjected to the harshest regimens of starvation and filth. That is where my grandfather and the others were marched to and arrived at before dawn on December 13.

Two shacks cordoned off in Camp C opened in May 1941, after the non-aggression pact between the USSR and Germany broke down and the Nazis invaded Soviet territory. White and Red Russians arrested on French soil were kept here.[37]

The French, Americans, and Russians were malnourished, but they were fed something, and they could receive letters, packages, and visitors. This was not the case in the Jewish Camp. It was as severe as other Nazi camps, as it was the only one in France under direct control of the Germans at that time, before they also took charge of the camp at Drancy in 1943. Royallieu-Compiègne served, above all, as a place to punish the political opponents of the Reich, the Communist "agitators," and the Russians they had captured after the German invasion of Russia in August 1941; but it would become most notable for the suffering inflicted here on the Jewish prisoners.

Camp B and Camp C no longer exist. Today the spot they occupied is the site of a hospital, although Camp C also extended beyond what is now the present-day border of Compiègne; that land now hosts quaint homes with gardens and tricycles on their lawns. Thus it would be difficult to describe the nightmare that my grandfather and his companions lived through, were it not for the personal accounts that survived.

Their conditions of imprisonment were even more tragic because the Jewish Camp was kept a secret during the first two months of its existence. The families had no idea where their relatives were. The Jewish prisoners were forbidden to write or receive letters, and they could not get packages. It was only due to the generosity and aid of the French political prisoners and imprisoned Russian citizens that a few packages and letters made it through to Camp C—at least until late January 1942, when the Germans got wind of this strategy and the number of packages received in the French Communist and Russian camps was restricted.

Each building, or block, of the Jewish Camp contained several rooms with separate bunks. At six meters wide and fifteen to sixteen meters long, each room was originally designed to hold up to sixteen French soldiers. The German authorities, though, fitted out each room in the Jewish Camp to hold thirty to thirty-five Jewish French prisoners.

For the first month, the men slept on straw mats, three centimeters thick—scarcely more than an inch—thick, placed directly on the cement floor; there was no other furniture. Around January 13, 1942, they were given bed frames with meager mattresses, so thin that the iron springs bruised their emaciated bodies.

But I am going too quickly. It is one a.m. on December 13, when my grandfather and the others arrive at the camp. According to Serge Klarsfeld's account, that morning there were 390 merchants and company directors, 322 artisans, 91 engineers, 63 doctors and dentists, 33 pharmacists and chemists, 31 students, 27 professionals, 16 lawyers, 11 professors, and 53 with no known profession.

The windows are broken and let in the freezing cold air. During this winter of 1941–1942, the temperature hovers at around 20 degrees below zero Celsius—minus 4 degrees Fahrenheit. In the middle of the room sits a wood-burning stove that can fit logs of up to one and a half meters long, but much of what the men are given has to be cut down to size, without a saw; this allows them meager heat for just two hours a day. No light either, at least not for the first few weeks, so they sit in darkness for between sixteen and seventeen hours a day, confined, with nothing to occupy their minds. Arguments keep breaking out between those who choose to have heat from the stove and endure the choking smoke and those who would prefer not to use the stove and endure the icy air. Where is Léonce Schwartz's straw mat? Near the stove, forcing him to breathe in the fumes? Or is he among the ones near the doors and windows, more exposed to the wet and cold?

Each room is supervised by a leader chosen by the Jewish prisoners themselves. Their task is to keep order, to make sure the sweeping and emptying of bedpans is kept up, and to make sure all the men are present at roll call, twice a day.[38] These leaders, out of sheer exhaustion, will often pass the baton after just a few weeks. They, in turn, are supervised by the block leader, who is in charge of distributing the "meals." Block leaders are appointed by the Nazi higher-ups. They live outside the camp and rarely see the prisoners; their only qualification seems to be that they know how to speak German. Many of them are generous, sharing, making sure that each man receives his ration of food. Others are mean or conniving, taking more than their share of the food.

It is December 16, three days after the prisoners arrived, and Hauptsturmführer Dannecker, with his neuroses and many tics, has come to the camp. Sonderführer Kuntze,[39] the true head of the camp, leads the way. The *Sonderführer* speaks French, more or less, having once been a waiter in a café in Montmartre and, most likely, a member of the

French Fifth Column, a group of spies in the pay of the Nazis. The wardens are next in the line of command. Two of them, Erich Jäger and Andreas Schröder, have already been nicknamed *hommes-chiens,* "human dogs," by the prisoners. Their photos are displayed in the garden of the camp: smiling, calm, each with a small mustache and each wearing a flat cap; they don't appear to be as cruel as their nicknames warn.

The head German medical officer at Frontstalag 122, Major Furtwängler, a distinguished, elegant-looking man capable of a rare type of cruelty, announces that the invalids must gather together, and then he shows his "sense of humor" by repeating what General Otto von Stülpnagel had said two just days before[40] of his Jewish Bolshevik criminals: "A bad heart? Excellent for the Russian front!" and "Crippling rheumatism? Nothing better than the Russian climate to get cured." Nevertheless, days later, on December 18 and 20, under a special order, seventy-three prisoners considered to be gravely ill and twenty more who are over sixty-five are freed, along with fifteen others. Liberating groups of men like this will be the exception for the next three months. Instead, certain individuals will be freed, often men in such bad health that the

Germans prefer to see them die in the hospital, because death in this camp of *einflussreiche Juden,* influential Jews, is not looked upon well by the Vichy government. And at this time, that still counts for something.

One of the prisoners' first discoveries is the camp's privy. The toilets are housed in a brick building approximately six meters long by one to one and a half meters wide. There are spots for the men to place their feet on the sides of five small holes, a humiliatingly insufficient number for a thousand prisoners. Wind sweeps through the privy, making it constantly cold; the filth is disgusting, and the smell abominable. Going to the toilet means true physical and mental suffering, so constipation will become a safeguard to such an extent that bowel obstructions have to be cared for as emergencies in the infirmary, or until exhaustion and illness give the prisoners uncontrollable dysentery. The sink to wash in is just as putrid: a stone trough, used as a urinal at night, has a thin stream of freezing cold water flowing from a spout, except on days when the old pipes freeze and not a drop comes out of the tap.

Discussions among the prisoners quickly focus on finding a balance between cleanliness and the cold. The dilemma: those who wash themselves completely are liable to get sick, and those who wash themselves too little risk getting pleurisy.

The lack of sanitation very quickly causes vermin to appear. Lice infest straw mats and multiply through dirty clothes. Because of the constant scratching, the prisoners' bodies are soon covered in wounds. Their clothes will be disinfected, or so they are told. At the same time they will be allowed, just once in three months, to go to the showers located in the Russian camp. There, six men at a time stand for a few minutes under a single showerhead before putting on their clothes, which at best have been only poorly cleaned, if at all, and are still full of lice; this does away with any meager comfort the showers might provide.

My grandfather, like the others, has brought very few pairs of underwear and not many clothes. After a few days, given the lack of soap, the underwear worn day and night becomes soiled. The business suits too thin to withstand the cold and the lack of socks and solid shoes make for more suffering. Frostbite happens quite quickly. Left without treatment, fissures turn into open wounds or edemas, making the prisoners' hands and feet swell, and threaten to turn gangrenous. Moreover, the roll calls, twice a day in the snow, morning and evening, with their feet only somewhat covered, cause some of the men to faint from the pain. Those too sick to report have exemptions from the block leaders of the barracks, but sometimes lower-ranking German officers come inside anyway, kick over the flimsy bed frames, beat those prisoners, and force them outside in their bare feet.

"*Raus! Raus!*" These shouts ordering the men to get out quickly become familiar. The roll calls last from three-quarters of an hour to two and a half hours, including several head counts that never tally the same way, and always end with the prisoners of the Jewish Camp waiting outside for a very long time, whatever the weather, while the roll call has been completed in the other quarters at Royallieu-Compiègne.

Along with the cold and the filth, starvation is the third weapon in the German armory to transform these inmates into ghosts. At eight o'clock in the morning, they are given only a disgusting drink. The prisoners jokingly call it "Boldo."[41] Its sole merit is that it is hot.

A routine is established. At one in the afternoon, they receive the soup of the day. Its consistency is acceptable for the first two days of their imprisonment, but very soon it becomes thinner and thinner: made of a liquid of some kind with a few turnips or carrots, some barley and split peas. Sometimes, a piece of meat the size of a nut floats on top of a man's portion. A loaf weighing under two pounds is shared among six men, along with half an ounce of margarine or jam, and is meant to last until the next day. Still, it is the daily treasure. At five o'clock, hot "tea" for the evening arrives, though it is not much different from that morning's Boldo.

It's no surprise that food becomes an obsession.

To understand the meaning of Frontstalag 122, it is essential to read the personal journals written by many of the men imprisoned there. The majority of the diaries that survived and are quoted here have been published, for the most part, by the Sons and Daughters of Jewish Deportees from France or by the Foundation for the Memory of the Shoah.

Take the diary of François Montel, for instance. He arrived at Royallieu-Compiègne later than most of the original 743 "prominent Jews," but he suffered the same agonies, having come from Drancy and then sent back there before his final deportation to Auschwitz, where he died in August 1943. He was a remarkable man. A brilliant lawyer and the author of several collections of poetry, he demonstrated his bravery in June 1940 when he volunteered to fight for France. Not long after, he was taken prisoner in Germany. Although he was set free the next year, in March 1941, he was arrested only a few months later, during the *rafle* of August 20–23, 1941, along with another forty or so Jewish lawyers.[42]

Reading his journal, published together with Georges Kohn's (discussed later), moved me deeply as I was beginning to understand that mental strength comes from mysterious sources. This man, like certain other prisoners in Frontstalag 122, also had exceptional moral strength. He took solace from literature, writing passionately about André Gide, François Villon, and Gérard de Nerval,[43] as well as about daily life under Saint Louis IX, king of France from 1226 to 1270. "What he had within him was stronger than what was beaten out of him. François Montel was crushed, but he wasn't defeated," writes Serge Klarsfeld in his introduction to the writings of this remarkable man.[44]

The dentist Benjamin Schatzman's journal is another example, though one very different in tone. Arrested on December 12, he was first sent seventy kilometers from Paris to Royallieu-Compiègne, then to Drancy, in the northeastern part of Paris, and from there to Pithiviers and Beaune-la-Rolande, both in north-central France, before finally being deported to Auschwitz. His testimony contains a mass of information and emotional outpourings, describing in extensive, minute detail the lack of food and the harm to bodily functions the starvation caused. He not only kept a journal during his captivity in France—which ends tragically with his final entry as he threw the journal from a deportation train at Chalon-sur-Saône—but he also compiled notes that provide a wealth of insight to help us understand what life was like in the concentration camps.

Concerning the food at Frontstalag 122, Dr. Schatzman wrote that the prisoners were constantly tormented by hunger. "I'm living in a continual state of needing to eat. It follows that my thoughts are constantly focused on nourishing my body. . . . It is a true struggle and a wrench to stop eating this bread. Not only do I wait for it with painful impatience, with a feeling of dizziness, but I find it enormously difficult to stop myself from eating it because I absolutely must leave some for the next day's morning and noontime. But just imagine the feeling when I tell you that the quantity given was barely enough to taste it!"[45]

In the letters that escaped via Russian and French prisoners at Royallieu-Compiègne and were then delivered to these men's families, and in the requests for packages that arrived in dribs and drabs by the same means, the detainees begged for medical supplies. But their correspondence detailed in particular their paltry diets, and their wish lists for things like sardines, chocolates, or even pieces of bread made them dream of receiving imaginary packages. Though receiving real ones had become rarer and rarer.

François Mauriac, clearly moved, wrote a review in 1946 of the French playwright Jean-Jacques Bernard's book on his persecution, in which he describes the camp as one "with no forced labor, no physical torture, no exterminations, but [where] the executioner remained invisible: all they had to do was let their victims gradually die of hunger."[46,47] And Serge Klarsfeld emphasized this point: "Hunger and illness had the same devastating effect [in

Frontstalag 122] as in the camps in Poland. But [it was] unique in occupied Europe in not having an active policy of extermination, and where there was a population who was more or less equally well-educated, [thus] Compiègne was a camp where a lot was written. It was one of the only ways to avoid going mad."[48]

The general opinion of those who survived was that the solidarity between the Russians and the French prisoners was the sole reason, initially, why the number of Jewish deaths here was limited to about forty victims during the three months of their detention, without counting the number of deteriorated men evacuated to the hospital, where they died, or the ones who died at home soon after they had been liberated.

Resourcefulness, helped along by luck, allowed some of the wives of the men arrested in the *rafle* of December 12, 1941, to find where their husbands were being held. For many long weeks, my grandmother Marguerite knew nothing about where Léonce was, and she looked for clues all over France to find the only man she'd ever loved, who'd been taken away in the middle of the night. Like her neighbor Mariette Engelmann, my grandmother finally received some information that allowed her to pinpoint the camp at Royallieu-Compiègne. From there she tried to reach a few people who might have links to the French government, though clearly she was not the only one: Vichy was overwhelmed with desperate pleas.

According to the historian Laurent Joly, the *rafle* of prominent Jews was a shock even to the collaborationist Vichy government, which had wanted to protect their former Jewish soldiers and not "upset the old French Jews"—as Admiral François Darlan[49] called them—who had been assimilated for a long time.[50] The admiral clearly understood the risk: the general public could be outraged by the arrest of long-standing French citizens, regardless of their faith. Besides, there were social connections between power brokers in the Vichy government and the elites of the French social circles who'd been arrested in the *rafle*.[51]

Even Xavier Vallat,[52] commissioner-general for Jewish questions in wartime Vichy, voiced his objection, but to no avail. He requested that the former soldiers and older men taken in the *rafle* be freed. The Gestapo refused. Moreover, only Fernand de Brinon, number three in the Vichy regime and its representative to the German High Command in Paris, was given permission to formally petition the occupying authorities for the rare release of certain men.[53] To Commissioner-General Vallat, as well as to historians Michael Marrus, Robert Paxton, and Laurent Joly, this *rafle* was a "grave psychological error" that sapped Vichy's efforts toward a more "favorable climate for anti-Semitism."[54] He and Admiral Darlan thought it counterproductive to attack assimilated French Jews while there were so many foreign Jews in the Free Zone.[55] But the *rafle* also proved to be a turning point that induced the French state to harden its stance against foreign Jews and convince the Germans to get rid of them.[56]

Yet Frontstalag 122 was not under Vichy authority but under the direct military administration of the Wehrmacht. The Gestapo, commanded by Hauptsturmführer Dannecker, had the authority to decide whether prisoners would be released. To be clear, those in the Wehrmacht, whom revisionists may present as being "kind soldiers of the regular army,"[57] were hardly better than the cruel SS or the Gestapo.

Léonce Schwartz, my grandfather, before the war.

My grandparents Léonce and Marguerite.

Arrival at Frontstalag 122, Royallieu-Compiègne.

Frontstalag 122.

Frontstalag 122.

Jewish prisoners being transferred from Frontstalag 122, on March 19, 1942, to the camp at Drancy. Most were later deported to Auschwitz.

PARIS . HOPITAL . VAL . de . GRACE

REGISTRE . ENTRÉES . Jours Pairs

14.2.42 au 18.6.42 | TERRITOIRE |

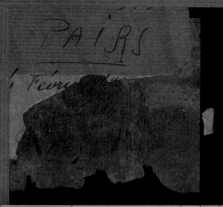

PAIRS

				Nom		
1505	1ère Division Sanitaire Volontaire	bataillon ou escadron.	comp° ou batter°.	Kozlorowski albi	2d.	3m
1506	art 64	bataillon ou escadron.	comp° ou batter°.	Brec Edmond	2d.	4m
1507	int civil	bataillon ou escadron.	comp° ou batter°.	King Edouard	ameri	MC
1508	— id —	bataillon ou escadron.	comp° ou batter°.	Schroartz Leon	français	MC
1509	Secret. d'état Aviation	bataillon ou escadron.	comp° ou batter°.	Colin Emile	agt civil	LBL

OPPOSITE: The admissions register of the Val-de-Grâce hospital where Léonce Schwartz (spelled as Leon Schoartz) was transferred as a political prisoner on February 24, 1942.

ABOVE LEFT: Commemorative plaque at the Place de l'École Militaire, in memory of the 743 French Jews arrested on December 12, 1941, during the *rafle* of influential Jews and interned at Royallieu-Compiègne.

ABOVE RIGHT: Official posthumous confirmation that Léonce Schwartz was a political prisoner, addressed to my grandmother Marguerite in 1958.

A poignant drawing of my grandfather, wearing an armband with the number 3450, by a fellow prisoner at the Val-de-Grâce hospital.

3

LIVING AND DYING AT ROYALLIEU-COMPIÈGNE

Léonce Schwartz quickly understands that resistance against the enemy begins with the body, so it is necessary for him to maintain himself in as good a condition as possible for as long as possible, especially by adhering to a strict code of hygiene. His need for cleanliness is as indispensable as his need for walking or talking, which is a tall order when he has only a sliver of soap to share with friends, no matter how generous they might be; when there is not much underwear to change into; when the icy trickle of water in the trough that serves as a sink barely allows him to wash his socks, which, themselves, have become insufficient shields against frostbite, breeding cracks in his skin and other wounds inflicted by this year's freezing winter.

Though life in Frontstalag 122 is known to us today mostly through the prisoners' postwar narratives and correspondence, I found no letters at all that my grandfather managed to send to my grandmother Margot. Many others' letters, however, are preserved at the Mémorial de la Shoah in Paris, and they are poignant. The majority of those that survived and are quoted here were published by the Fondation pour la Mémoire de la Shoah, thanks to Serge Klarsfeld, who vowed to build what he termed in one of his writings "a monument made of paper."

The agonizing narrations of the men's three months of imprisonment are of two types. Some of the detainees chose to emphasize how they kept their spirits up, in part by telling of the irreproachable conduct and generosity of the great majority of their fellow prisoners. This was the stance taken by the playwright Jean-Jacques Bernard and the businessman Roger Gompel.[58] Though I wonder if this stemmed from a desire to provide a dignified, even idealized picture of their suffering in order to resist the way the Nazis tried to reduce them by making them live like animals, including in their most ordinary daily routines.

The second type of narrative, from those such as the dentist Benjamin Schatzman, as well as Henri Jacob-Rick and Georges Wellers,[59] aimed more at realism.

Dr. Schatzman's deeply moving narrative was tragically interrupted by his deportation to Auschwitz-Birkenau, where he died on September 28, 1942. Serge Klarsfeld describes him as "an exceptional man" in his introduction to the published journals, notes, correspondence, and *mémoires* of the doctor, whose ideas were of the highest order and whose life story was extraordinary.

Benjamin was born in Romania in 1877, and later he and his parents made *aliyah*[60] to Palestine, where he learned French in school. At the age of twenty, he went to France and became an agricultural engineer before returning to Palestine. Then, disillusioned, he emigrated to New Zealand. In 1905, at the age of twenty-eight, he returned to France and began studying to become a dentist. He went on to open a practice on the Rue des Courcelles in Paris, and made many important discoveries in his field, along with gaining French citizenship, marrying, and having three children; one of them was Evry Schatzman, who rose to become a famous astrophysicist.

In the two volumes of his *mémoires*,[61] Dr. Schatzman details at great length the suffering he was subjected to; his attempts to understand the psychology of his captors and of his fellow prisoners—for example, the harshness of his torturers and sometimes the egoism, even stupidity, of some of his peers, as well as his reflections on life, humanity, and happiness, which seems impossible in that other world he endured.

The merchant Henri Jacob-Rick[62] also writes of some of the men who seemed dubious: an outcast with shifty eyes; a father and his son-in-law who bickered constantly; a rich man described as a *"poseur fini"*—a complete fraud; a salesman of God knows what who had sold food back on the black market for a higher price; and those who fought over the *"rab"*—that is, the dregs left at the bottom of a soup bucket.

Saül Castro, a Jew of Turkish origin and a naturalized French citizen, also describes such fights, which sometimes erupted over food: "They lunge for it like starving wolves, a horrifying sight, unworthy of a human being.

Starvation held a grip to such an extent that they would do anything for a bit of bread."[63]

As time passed, several prisoners, in fact, described an atmosphere in which each man thought only of himself. According to Georges Wellers, twenty or so individuals behaved badly. He writes: "Thieves distribute food taken from others. They shamefully traffic in what we needed to survive. They are men of weak character who have given in to egoism."[64]

In most of the testimonies, however, certain names continue to emerge: the names of men whose behavior was admired by everyone. Pierre Masse is almost unanimously cited as an admirable figure during those atrocious months of their captivity.[65] Kind, committed, and calm, he even organized a courtroom with other jurists to try to settle conflicts that arose in the barracks.

Pierre Masse had been arrested in August, along with other Jewish lawyers, and was sent first to Drancy. He was then transferred to Royallieu-Compiègne shortly after the December 12 *rafle*. There he found his brother, Roger Masse, a graduate of the École Polytechnique and a colonel in the French army, who had been taken prisoner, freed, and then rearrested in the *rafle*.[66] The two brothers left an impression on the other prisoners as being great men. They came from a family in which "everyone shared the idea of service to France and a love of the Republic to the highest degree," as Robert Badinter, a former minister of justice under French president François Mitterrand, wrote in his moving homage.[67]

Pierre Masse had already stood up to and against the enactment of a law in October 1940 that specifically forbade Jews from serving as military officers. In a famous letter to the then president of the Council of Ministers, Maréchal Pétain, he wrote:

> I would be obliged if you could tell me if I must go and remove the stripes from my brother's uniform; he was a Second Lieutenant in the 36th Infantry Regiment, killed at Douaumont in April 1916; or my son-in-law's stripes, a Second Lieutenant in the 14th Cavalry Regiment, killed in Belgium in May 1940; or J. P. Masse's stripes, my nephew, Lieutenant in the 23rd Colonial army, killed at Rethel in May

1940? May my brother keep the Military Medal he was awarded at Neuville St. Vaast, that I buried him with? . . .

P. MASSE

FORMER CAPTAIN IN THE
36TH INFANTRY REGIMENT,
AWARDED THE LEGION OF HONOR
AND THE CROIX DE GUERRE,
FORMER UNDERSECRETARY OF STATE
AT THE DEPARTMENT OF MILITARY JUSTICE[68]

Though I haven't yet found any sign of my grandfather in the narratives left by other prisoners from their three long months together at Frontstalag 122,[69] the motto of the Schwartz family is to grit your teeth and show strength of character; so I would like to imagine that he carried himself in an exemplary manner.

Many of the men also paint a laudatory picture of René Blum—brother of Léon Blum. A man of the theater, and a founder and director of the Ballets de Monte-Carlo, he came back to France after her defeat by the Nazis in 1940, when he could have safely remained in New York City. "I am too well-known and belong to a family that is too famous to even think of fleeing from the Germans or seeking protection from those in the Vichy government," he declared with panache.[70] Many narratives cite him as always trying, even when he was very weak, to comfort anyone he felt was worse off than himself.

Yet, because political divisions continued, some men opposed to his brother's Popular Front government held a grudge against the whole Blum family, blaming them for all the misfortunes in the French Third Republic and its demise to the Vichy regime.[71] Though there were very few men at Royallieu-Compiègne who held that view, this rift was an example of how Vichy's deceitful, guilt-inducing rhetoric had seeped in. This was the case for Henri Jacob-Rick, who found the impresario "enormously loquacious. I argued with him saying that we could put a lot on his brother for us being here."[72]

René Blum was among the prisoners transferred to Drancy on March 19, 1942, then deported to Auschwitz, along with most of the other men captured in the December 12 *rafle*; he died there in September 1942. Georges Wellers cites friends who had told him that the Germans had singled out René and taken him off the train at

Auschwitz-Birkenau.[73] Witnesses who returned from that hell reported that this man of such exceptional quality was believed to have been thrown alive into a crematorium.

The imprisoned Jewish doctors at Frontstalag 122 were also unanimously lauded for their gentleness, kindness, and dedication. Dr. Robert Netter[74] and Dr. Gaston Neumann, who worked in the infirmary, were described by patients as being selfless.

They worked under Major Furtwängler, a person all the prisoners recognized as a sadist. His motto was, "I am first an anti-Semite, then a Nazi, then a doctor." He refused to evacuate the men who were sick, except in the most extreme cases. Yet these Jewish doctors, among them Dr. Netter and Dr. Neumann, were so moved by the horrendous state of some of the prisoners that they took the risk of alerting the camp authorities to their patients' plight. For this they were sentenced to prison by Major Furtwängler—yes, there was even a prison inside this camp of torture—with him stating that they had "allowed their comrades to die." Moreover, when the doctors asked for clemency for certain very sick patients, Major Furtwängler refused, advising "undernourishment until the end." *The end of what?*

But of all the men at Frontstalag 122, the generosity of the Russian and French Communist prisoners there received the greatest praise. They took every sort of risk to help sneak through some packages and smuggle mail in and out as well, seemingly adopting the Jewish prisoners as their own.

The historian Adam Rutkowski, to whom much is owed for his 1981 study of Frontstalag 122, which produced topographies and lists of the sick and deported,[75] pays homage to the Russian Abraham Alpérine, and to Georges Cogniot,[76] who had degrees in literature, was the editor of the newspaper *L'Humanité*, and served as the head of Camp A, the French Camp. He organized and ran a program encouraging his prison mates to read literature and to learn about other types of art and culture, up until his escape in June 1942.

Messieurs Alpérine and Cogniot came to the aid of Camp C with courage and kindness, even risking their own lives to create a system to help the Jewish prisoners. For example, their smuggling took place when night fell, near the barbed wire fences, where they tossed tins of sardines, cookies, and dried fruit to those in the Jewish Camp. This was very much appreciated, even though it barely eased the hunger of these men, who were otherwise reduced to rummaging through garbage cans, hoping to find discarded orange peels from which they might suck some sustenance.

The day passes slowly, so slowly. Some of the prisoners play bridge, while others try to care for their frostbite, which is getting worse. The conversations turn endlessly around possible liberation, fueled by rumors, which circulate quickly in this microcosm far from the rest of the world—especially rumors of imminent release, although in the days that follow, all of them will prove to be false hopes. But for these men, for now, only a short time after the *rafle* that has led to their arrests, there is the certainty that their ordeal will be over quickly. There is even a rumor that the Russians have already taken back Kiev, and that the end is near.[77]

Other rumors begin to circulate too, ones much feared, of "departures to the East," though nobody knows exactly what that means. Questions torment these men, who up until now have been protected in life but have now been "thrown," as Serge Klarsfeld will note, "into freezing cold barracks where people [are] starved, before going to die in a gas chamber at the other end of Europe." They spend their time wondering—especially in these beginning hours here—what they have done to deserve such a cruel fate.

A matter of days, weeks, say the optimists. But as the calendar moves on, they continue to obsess over food, chewing their pitiful turnips, scraping their bowls for any bits of vegetables stuck at the bottom. They see themselves, almost as if standing in front of a mirror, in the latrines, where each man observes his own deterioration in the bodies of the others. Their bodies: naked, horrifically growing thinner and thinner, with neither fat nor muscle clinging to their skeletons. Their stained bandages, and their ever-increasing weakness; their pessimism taking hold even while they understand that giving in means death. But they do not have the strength to fight.

In the face of this torment whose finality he foresees, Dr. Schatzman feels his own resignation; but at the same time, he denounces surrendering his will in January 1942: "To resign oneself is to abandon one's dignity." Everyone tries to cling to the hope of their liberation, especially those who are older—Dr. Schatzman is nearly sixty-five, but he lucidly perceives the systematic extermination, and he is determined to reflect on the reasons for the barbarous treatment the Germans inflict on the Jews. Seeing the ravages of starvation at a time when he does not yet know of gas chambers, when until only days before gas chambers did not yet exist,[78] he understands that the goal is to destroy them. He says that he and his fellow prisoners are destined to become "garbage." He also does not know that this word will run throughout the French deportations of Jews: used by the anti-Semite Pierre Laval to describe foreign Jews, it reappears under the pen of the victims themselves to describe their plight, such as the writer Robert Antelme, who was deported to Buchenwald, while Primo Levi, deported to Auschwitz, will use other words such as "worms," "rags," "the damned."

During a miraculous reprieve of working for five weeks in the infirmary, Dr. Schatzman watches with horror the cruel medical treatment that leads to an unforgettable amount of patient misery and torment. This moves him to make an accusation: "Why are these people being handed over by our French state with no apparent resistance at all? It is impossible to either understand or forgive." His words definitively echo those of his prison mate Roger Gompel, the head administrator of the Parisian luxury department store Aux Trois Quartiers and a former combatant in the First World War, during which he was seriously wounded and awarded many military decorations: "How many Frenchmen, out of sordid calculation or simple cowardice, have become the complaisant agents or silent accomplices of such atrocities? Such betrayal has been painfully felt as one of the ignoble stains of our defeat."

Even sparse but precious news from their families, which some manage to have smuggled in, no longer provides comfort. But then, on January 28, 1942, permission is given allowing them correspondence. The authorities distribute postcards for the prisoners to send to their families: they can ask for clothing, but not for food or medicine. Yet it is only cruel cynicism: the cards are never sent; they are instead used to feed the stoves keeping the Germans warm. About six weeks later, on March 12, a few days before the men's scheduled release from Royallieu-Compiègne, letters are officially allowed.

It is astonishing to discover, in this atmosphere, amid this ordeal, the intense cultural life here. At least now, at the beginning, from late December to the end of January, in any case—until their weakness becomes too debilitating for some of them to even get out of bed.

There is a lecture held almost every evening in some of the barracks, with the men huddling around the stove before the light from its flames fades. The lecturers, with neither paper nor pencils, give talks about their specialties to the prisoners still strong enough to stand up, while the weakest ones sit on beds nearby, trying to listen in; all of this is an extraordinary and surprising initiative that bears witness to the intellectual quality of these prisoners. The talks help the lecturers keep their minds from atrophying, and help their audiences forget their present stations for at least an hour.

Some of the most popular subjects are the life of Blaise Pascal, and specific aspects of art, agriculture, the oil industry, accounting, and the potential of science. Louis Engelmann gives a class on electricity; René Blum speaks about the French men of letters Alphonse Allais, Tristan Bernard, and Georges Courteline;[79] Jean-Jacques Bernard talks about the theater and French poetry of the Middle Ages; André Ullmo, about the greatest trials in the Court of Justice; Jacques Ancel about the concept of nations.

Two subjects are forbidden, though: Germany, for fear of *mouchards*, snitches; and the "Jewish Question."

At the heart of Frontstalag 122's uniqueness was a false assumption. The *rafle* had intentionally targeted a group of some seven hundred Jews that the Germans assumed would be homogeneous. In fact, there was an element of strong division, detailed with great intensity by Jean-Jacques Bernard, in particular, as well as by the historians Georges Wellers[80] and Adam Rutkowski.[81]

Among the assimilated "Israelites," as with the majority of French Jews who had been integrated into French society for a long time, there was a deep desire to feel entirely French. I use the term "Israelite"[82] intentionally, though today it is only used derogatorily by shameful anti-Semites. The word "Jew" was not widely used at the time, except by the Germans and their sympathizers. Finding themselves the victims of other Frenchmen added even more agony to the prisoners' incomprehension of the situation they were in, and further complicated their sense of pride and duty in service to their country, as many of them were veterans and even former officers in the army. They had not, or had only very rarely, suffered from anti-Semitism in their adult lives; for the most part, these 743 men were not observant and did not go to synagogue; some had even married women who were not Jewish. They refused to see themselves as "Jews" and were offended by those who considered them to have an attributed identity apart from their place in French society. And if they considered themselves Jewish at all, it was more out of family tradition than religious calling.

Today, eighty years later, their surprise back then seems all the more astonishing since the law regarding the status of Jews in October 1940 had already caused them to be ostracized as never before since the ancien régime.[83] What's more, the period in the 1930s had been preceded by an increasing climate of anti-Semitism and by their own awareness of the much-talked-about *Mein Kampf*, the doctrines and writings of Adolf Hitler, published in France in 1934.[84]

The differences were even greater between the 743 Jewish prisoners arrested in the *rafle* and the other 300 Jewish prisoners, foreigners for the most part. The latter group of men had sought refuge in France following persecution in eastern and central Europe, having long suffered in pogroms, or from anti-Semitism. Arriving in France, they had hoped they could be safe, had hoped they could raise their children with a love of their new homeland; yet on the cusp of a world war, they spoke bitterly about France and blamed her, not just for leaving them unprotected but also for having given them a poor welcome even before handing them over to the Germans, the "Boches," as they called the occupiers.[85] Through the horrible betrayal of the Vichy government, they once again encountered the persecution they had known in the countries they'd been born in and from which they'd fled, and had not the slightest illusion that being Jewish meant anything other than being the targets of hatred from the anti-Semites and the Nazis' desire to eliminate them.

But the true heart of the difference between the prisoners lay in their reactions to their Judaic heritage. As Serge Klarsfeld notes, for "the assimilated, patriotic Jews who wished to believe they had only been arrested because they were suspected of being anti-German," this experience was both a scandalous and unspeakable indignation.[86] This group represented, therefore, the archetype of

French "Israelites," including former officers in the French army and even those decorated by the republic, caught up in a *rafle* sown with motivations and risks beyond their comprehension. My grandfather, for example, had been awarded the highest French order of merit, the Ordre National de la Légion d'Honneur, the Legion of Honor, of which he was very proud and which symbolized a great deal at the time to Jews who were worried about their integration into the life of the nation. The others, the foreigners, the fatalists, accustomed to ghettos and bigotry, mocked the blindness of their French countrymen and saw in their arrest the continuation of an age-old curse linked to their Jewish identity.

This divide happened to such an extent that a "social order struggle"—if I dare use the term—at Royallieu-Compiègne was surely brought on by the differences in status between the privileged Frenchmen of the professional echelons and the refugees, who were often artisans and clearly thought of less favorably, but most especially it was due to the great disparity between their respective forms of Judaism. As Louis Engelmann wrote in his journal, "There were as many differences between a Romanian

Jew and myself as between an Orthodox Romanian and an Aryan Frenchman."

Some of the influential men were even harsh and scornful toward the foreign Jews. Others, however, were intrigued. For instance, Roger Gompel, the businessman who traded in luxury goods and who, according to his writings, was a well-educated man, was astonished to discover a world unknown to him upon hearing those underprivileged prisoners singing songs in Yiddish in the evening, and found them very beautiful. Jean-Jacques Bernard made the contrast even more clear in his journal: "Like me, my companions only knew how to think as Frenchmen. They didn't know how to think as Jews."[87]

Jewish identity was such an issue here that in the evenings, some lectures got out of control when the subject was brought up. The peaceful and courteous Jacques Ancel grew angry when someone questioned him about the existence of a "Jewish state." As for Édouard Laemlé, the president of the Court of Appeals of Paris, he firmly rejected the idea of a Jewish community and adopted what would become a Sartrean definition of Judaism (even before Jean-Paul Sartre), proclaiming, "We are Jewish only from the moment when we are reproached for being Jewish." As to which side my grandfather took, what I do know about him leads me to believe that he shared the feelings of the Frenchmen who were simultaneously Jewish and secular, refusing to be defined by their practice, or not, of Judaism.

4

CHANGING FORTUNES

Beginning around mid-February 1942, conditions at the camp deteriorated more and more quickly, and even the prisoners who had avoided wallowing in their grievances were anxious about the Nazis' real objective for them. For example, Dr. Schatzman, who a month earlier had tested his resignation to death and found that premise far-fetched, nevertheless kept the idea of mass extermination in the back of his mind, vacillating: "The majority of us did not doubt that we were destined to be destroyed." However, according to the editors who annotated Dr. Schatzman's *mémoires,* to him that outcome "was so terrible and seemed so unimaginable that afterward he sought other possibilities. But during those days in the winter of 1942, the idea did occur to him, even if for only a moment."

Henri Jacob-Rick also understood the unimaginable. "We are up against a profound desire to do evil, which rips us away from the world of the living," he wrote to his wife in February. His heartbreaking letter can be seen in one of the interactive displays at the memorial in Royallieu-Compiègne.

It's a wonder how these men could possibly not think of death. Even the strongest and youngest had been unable to avoid deteriorating terribly. Their stabbing hunger brought with it dizziness, disorientation, and physical degradation that "by degrees, reduced men to animals," as Roger Gompel wrote. He added, with lucidity, that it was "a remorseless march toward death, using a method designed to humiliate, vilify, overwhelm, and exhaust [us] until the complete extinction of any human characteristic, [. . . in] a kind of cold-blooded pogrom."[88] The image is chilling,[89] but it deftly illustrates the prisoners' slow agony.

Those who left Frontstalag 122, either by being deported to Auschwitz or elsewhere, managing to escape into hiding, getting sent to the hospital, or being released due to unrecoverable frailty or imminent death, would depart having lost twenty-five to thirty kilos (fifty-five to sixty-five pounds) in their three months there. The malnutrition, the cold, and illness had begun to transform them into ghosts of their former selves. Records show that a prisoner's body temperature was often close to 34 or 35 degrees Celsius (93 to 95 degrees Fahrenheit); this is at the edge of hypothermia. It went up to 36.5°C (97.7°F) when they had a fever. And when it went down to 33.5°C (92.3°F), the end was near.

The Red Cross never managed to lessen the misery of the Jewish prisoners, either. In fact, the leaders of the humanitarian organization were regularly challenged about their attitudes toward Jews during the Second World War, though this was in part due to the limitations of their neutrality; yet they were equally suspected of deliberate indifference toward the fate of these Jewish prisoners and, more specifically, of not having warned the Jews of Paris of the mass arrests that would take place on July 16 and 17, 1942, the event known as the *rafle du Vél' d'Hiv.*[90] In any case, Red Cross personnel were never permitted to enter the Jewish Camp, even though they went into and out of the other camps at Royallieu-Compiègne.

The rations of food the Jewish prisoners were receiving continued to get smaller too, which led, as already described, to stoicism or fights. As a treat, each man might get a cookie or a date, or on a special day, a nugget of sugar to be shared among six men. Roger Gompel writes: "For the Jews, no pity! We were truly treated worse than animals, but without having even the ASPCA concerned with our fate."

Echoing that distress, Saül Castro refers to the infirmary as the "House of the Cripples." It was infested with lice, but more food was provided there than in the barracks. Either way, the terrifying and disgraceful treatment of the Jewish prisoners was still seen starkly. He writes: "Starvation is wreaking havoc, our torturers are causing us to die very slowly. . . . I can see myself dying more each day. . . . Our eyes look haunted and are bulging out of their sockets; if this continues much longer, we'll end up going mad."[91]

During this period, the cogs in the Germans' extermination machinery were still moving slowly. But that would soon change. On January 20, 1942, at the Wannsee Conference, SS Officer Reinhard Heydrich[92] presented the Reich authorities with "the Final Solution to the Jewish Question in Europe"—in more brutally direct words, the practical, concrete elements needed to carry out the mass extermination of Jews. As the historian Adam Rutkowski explains: "This was the moment when, in Berlin, the move from a policy of social elimination to a strategy of physical elimination was being prepared. The *rafle* of December 12th took place just as this shift was happening."

Moreover, since the *rafle* that caught my grandfather and so many others had been approved by the führer himself, it is highly likely, notes the historian Laurent Joly,[93] "that its timing coincided with Hitler's announcement to his inner circle regarding the total extermination of the Jews of Europe."

I would like to relate a very beautiful story told by Georges Wellers, a story I cannot read without getting a lump in my throat. In *From Drancy to Auschwitz*, his *mémoires*, he describes the heart-rending fate of a Russian Jew who was in the same block, if not the same barracks, as him. He became friends with this man, whom he described as having "a character of rare stature."[94]

He was named Rabinovitch,[95] and in the camp he quickly took on the nickname "Ritch," as that had been his name in the theater world. He'd been arrested at the Place de l'Étoile in the same *rafle* of prominent Jews on December 12, though as one of the other Jews picked up in the street as a means to meet the Nazi quota, and had been imprisoned without being allowed to collect any clothing or food. He had studied medicine, but upon leaving Russia after the 1917 revolution, he'd embarked on a wonderful career as an opera singer. He was known for his beautiful voice, his stately bearing, and his sweet nature, so refined and incredibly generous. His Russian friends bestowed small kindnesses upon him. But Ritch was embarrassed by this attention and endlessly pretended that he wasn't hungry so he could share those kindnesses, and the packages he received, by handing out most of them to the others in the Jewish Camp.

And, wishing to receive no special treatment, especially from one of his Jewish friends who was the head of the barracks and less scrupulous than him, he refused to accept the privilege of extra soup or bread that might have been "saved" from the rations of less-favored prisoners. He sacrificed himself more than anyone else, apologized for the few favors he received, and, in particular, joined the men who, at nightfall, would distribute the food that had been secretly passed to him by the Russians.

But his health deteriorated rather quickly. Ritch's feet were horribly frozen and swollen, and covered in deep cuts, which stayed raw, as there were no bandages or medicine. His situation was so dire, he couldn't put on his shoes, so using string, he instead placed his feet on top of them and tied them on. He was powerless in the face of the brutality and injustice. As he lost a considerable amount of weight, fell ill, and had a fever, he was barely able to keep getting up for the roll calls, and even fainted in the middle of some. Yet, the more he suffered, the more his attitude and generosity became admirable.

During the "lectures" around the stove given by those prisoners with specific talents, the men often asked Ritch to sing, but he declined, finding himself too weak. One evening, however, despite his frailty, he agreed to participate in a concert of sorts and to sing some Russian songs. With the beauty of his voice, so poignant, so touching, the power and gentleness emanating from within and then out through his emaciated body, he delighted his audience and moved them to tears.

On March 27, the day on which most of the prisoners were to be deported, Georges Wellers found Ritch among five hundred others. Suffering with a fever, he could barely stand up, but he was ready to board the train with a hallowed look on his face and a deep intensity in his eyes. "*Adieu tout le monde*," he whispered. "This will soon be over and I'm happy about it." He died on the train on the way to Auschwitz.

All the Jewish survivors of Frontstalag 122 were very careful not to compare their experiences, as terrible as they were, with the absolute horror of extermination camps, where suffering, torture, and death were much more systematically programmed. Moreover, after their liberation, when the Shoah was beginning to be known, this disturbing comparison of their horror against others' was one of the reasons for their restraint. Roger Gompel's daughter, who published her father's journal, explains their reticence very well:

> If, after the Liberation, my father decided not to publish his experiences, it was probably because by then, he had become aware—as we all had—of the fate the Jews faced in the death

camps, and he felt that his own ordeal had been less difficult to bear in comparison.[96,97]

In telling the story of the *rafle* and the camp, I too do not intend to make the prisoners at Royallieu-Compiègne seem more like martyrs than they actually were. What I am trying to do here is shed a bit more light on the history of a concentration camp in the shadows of Paris, run by the Germans and using the same system as in their French death camps in Drancy, Pithiviers, and Beaune-la-Rolande, but less known than those.

One of the questions that comes to mind when digging deep into this history is this: Why were the *einflussreiche Juden*, the influential Jews, arrested in the December 12, 1941, *rafle* not immediately deported? Or asked another way: Why was Frontstalag 122 used as a holding camp for them for three months?[98] An analysis of the documents is enlightening.

These men would seem to have been quite obviously marked for quick deportation, much sooner than March 27, 1942, which was the date when the first train left France—and Compiègne—with them aboard, en route to the death camps. According to an urgent secret telegram sent from Berlin on Christmas Eve 1941, the trains were already overloaded with German soldiers on leave during the holiday period, "which makes the transfer of a thousand Jews from France impossible."[99] A recommendation was therefore made by the Reich to temporarily hold the Jewish prisoners in a transit camp, until deportation in the spring.

Hauptsturmführer Dannecker was extremely aggravated by this delay, and went to Berlin himself at the end of February to try to persuade the man at the Gestapo in charge of the "Jewish Question," Adolf Eichmann, to change the decision set forth in his cable, which stated: "A thousand Jews will be taken into custody after the discussion about the timetable, and held in a hospitality (*sic*) camp located in the territory of the Reich."[100] In the end, on March 11, another telegram was sent from Berlin, this one announcing that "the departure of those thousand Jews, currently held in a camp at Compiègne, is scheduled for March 23, 1942, in a special train."[101] The *Hauptsturmführer* would adjust the date to four days later, March 27, and detail a plan for the prisoners' arrival at Auschwitz (he mentions the destination himself) on March 30 at dawn.[102]

Two further questions arise: Why were some of the prisoners authorized to be released? And why were only a portion of those authorizations carried out? It could be said that the ones who were freed were very often as a result of chance and a certain degree of German disorganization.

For example, on January 22, 1942, a report from the German military administration in France explained that the "commander of Camp C submitted a list of unfit Jews who were under eighteen or over fifty-five years old. Those Jews were to be freed, except in particular cases, if there were objections to their liberation; in those cases, they had to be transferred to the French internment camp at Drancy." Everything rested on the word "except," the decision belonging in the end to the Gestapo.

In fact, several lists were made of the men who were either too young or too old, which led to some of them being released. One of the first lists was made on December 17, 1941, five days after the *rafle,* and concerned the oldest men to be released. At the end of December, thirty-eight others considered to be gravely ill were also freed.

Months later, between March 12 and 15, 1942, those deemed to be "gravely ill"—around one hundred more men—were released. It is important to point this out in memory of so many tragically fated men who were less fortunate than my grandfather, who himself was spared only because he was among the gravely ill.

Some 550 of the men arrested in the December *rafle* would be deported directly from Compiègne to Auschwitz on March 27. "Convoy No. 767 left the Le Bourget-Drancy train station between 12:00 and 5:00 p.m. on the 27th, arrived at the Compiègne station at 6:40 p.m., and left again at 7:40 p.m. It arrived at Auschwitz on March 30, 1942, at 5:33 in the morning," Adam Rutkowski writes.[103] The schedule Hauptsturmführer Dannecker had laid out was adhered to.

As for another list with 178 deemed to be "unfit" for work, their lives were caught up in a third question, this one concerning a pseudo-regulation that excluded the young and the very old from deportation. There is every reason to believe that the Germans considered them to be more a matter of administrating the bureaucracy than of abiding by the rules since, in particular, three months after all the Jewish men had been removed from Frontstalag 122, in the summer of 1942, the Nazis would have no scruples about deporting both babies and the elderly. Royallieu-Compiègne was, in reality, a camp that supplied "forced labor" in the East. Thus, it seems logical to exclude those who were considered "unfit for labor" from the deportations to Auschwitz and other concentration camps, where they would be expected to "labor." Of course, "labor" was nothing more than a term to disguise genocide at a time when the Final Solution had been adopted just a few months earlier,[104] but had not yet risen to its deadliest efficiency. In March 1942, therefore, the young and the very old Jews arrested in the *rafle* were not at all of special concern to the Nazis; rather, their fates were more the result of a confused administration.

According to an account by Georges Kohn, on March 19, these 178 Jews (or 170 men on March 21, according to other accounts) under eighteen or over fifty-five were to be released from Royallieu-Compiègne. (The figures vary because it has been difficult for the survivors to reconstruct the experiences each of them lived.) Among them were Pierre Masse and his brother, Roger Masse, a colonel in the artillery division of the French army, who had been taken prisoner and had just been brought back from Germany in December.

When those men were taken from Frontstalag 122, they believed they were going to return to their families, but were abruptly disabused of that notion: the French police who took charge handcuffed the men to each other in units of two to transfer them to Drancy, which was still under French control. They would be deported a few days later to Auschwitz and other death camps. Marched on foot like convicts to the train station at Compiègne, these depleted souls, many of whom had been awarded the Legion of Honor, retraced their steps over the four or five kilometers they had walked that night three months before, as passersby watched with indignation and astonishment. Georges Kohn tells us that this was the only moment when Pierre Masse, that admirable man, "gave in." Handcuffed to Roger, he fought, tears in his eyes, insisting on respect for his brother's status as a patriotic soldier, outraged that these French police were giving support to the criminal Germans, especially against one of their own army's officers, sworn to defend them.[105]

French army prisoners, "prisoners of war," who had been sent to the front in 1939 and then captured, were still enlisted as active-duty soldiers in the military. But since the Geneva Convention made it clear that soldiers on active duty could not be deported, the Nazis often skirted the rules by having the enabling Vichy government deactivate these prisoners of war from all military service. The insane, tragic, and cruel hypocrisy of the Nazis to safeguard the appearance that they were abiding by the international protocols for the treatment of prisoners of war is astonishing. While pretending to respect the international pact to which their nation was a signatory, they sent these men to die in gas chambers, a crime of such monstrosity, breadth, and sophistication that it still remains unimaginable more than eighty years later.

As for releases of the one hundred gravely ill, these were carried out on a case-by-case basis. The head German medical officer at Royallieu-Compiègne, Major Furtwängler, reviewed each evaluation and refused to authorize the majority of them. Yet, as we know, certain of these men were freed. That was the case for my grandfather. But to tell more of that story, I have only distressing hypotheses.

I requested copies of the registers at the Val-de-Grâce hospital between February and March 1942, and once I received them, I pored through the arrivals and departures. Léonce Schwartz is listed as having been registered there as a "prisoner" on February 24. His name is found in a large handwritten directory, which shows it incorrectly spelled as "Leon Schoartz," but notes the correct address of his wife as 46 Rue de Tocqueville in Paris. The hospital officials had also added a category—which broke my heart, as I had never seen anything like it on a hospital register—describing him as an "Israelite." The reason for his hospitalization? "Tachycardia"—a benign choice of words, given the state in which he must have arrived, but this was, perhaps, the generic term given at that time for a heart condition contracted at Royallieu-Compiègne. Heart condition or not, once my grandfather was back on his feet, the Germans could have very well thrown him in with the others being herded off to the gas chambers. That was, in fact, what they often did with the seriously ill men.[106]

The person my grandfather shared a hospital room with at Val-de-Grâce made a portrait of him in his bed.[107] The sketch of my grandfather is dated March 13. I found it, almost by chance, among my parents' papers. This artistic drawing is poignant. He is sitting in a heavy coat that looks like a military greatcoat, wrapped in a blanket and wearing an armband with the number 3450, undoubtedly the identification assigned to him on December 12, 1941, the day of his arrest in the *rafle;* that number is also found in the hospital register. His face looks sunken, even though he had been better fed and looked after during the prior two weeks. He is holding his glasses in his hands. His eyes stare blankly, in despair.

Another of the rare documents in my possession is an official request my grandmother Margot made in 1957. She wanted to obtain a French government card in my grandfather's name confirming that he was a "political prisoner," which she did, and which has been verified in a copy of the dossier that the Ministry of Armed Forces provided to me. The information that my grandmother wrote out by hand also mentions other dates that have puzzled me for some time. She listed his admission into the Val-de-Grâce hospital as March 18, 1942, which contradicts the date on the register (February 24) and the portrait (March 13). In addition, she mentioned that he left on March 20, after only two days, when his true release was much later, on April 17. How could she have been mistaken about dates that surely were so important to her?

Serge Klarsfeld explained to me, with a gentle smile, that in order to have her husband officially classified as a "political prisoner"—which, however, did not provide a pension but did provide official recognition that he had been imprisoned—my grandmother must have changed the dates a little to conform to requirements proving that he had been incarcerated for a full three months. It is only of minor note, because even at the hospital his status was listed as "prisoner," a designation confirmed by the German authorities. And besides, the dossier, certified by a Colonel J. Henrion and dated August 5, 1957, that accorded my grandmother the government card attributed no importance to her dates and instead used the ones indicated on the hospital register. Was the colonel already working as a doctor at the time? If so, who was he?

Working in hospitals in 1939, and following the example of her own mother, Camille—who was so courageous in the First World War trenches on the Western Front at Verdun in 1916—Margot is said to have gotten Léonce out by slipping him into an ambulance, right under the noses of the soldiers guarding the hospital! For a long time, with the imagination of the adolescent I was then, I thought instead that her unbelievable courage had led her straight into the concentration camp. That story was heroic, but later on, I even fantasized further, deciding that in order to get into Frontstalag 122, she would have needed help, needed accomplices in the police or army ranks. It was a small leap from there to my imagining (in a romantic way) that she'd had a lover who had collaborated with the Germans but who had also helped save her Jewish husband, thus neatly wrapping everything up.

Today, all that remains are suppositions about my grandfather's escape. What happened afterward? Did they go back to their home at the Rue de Tocqueville, even though that would have been foolishly imprudent?

Considerably weakened by the months in captivity, forced to hide until the liberatiosn of Paris in late August 1944, and refusing to wear the *Judenstern,* the Jew's Star,[108] how is it that my grandfather found the strength to hold on until May 16, 1945? His passing was a week after the Armistice[109] and a few weeks after the return of his son, my father, from the Middle East, where he had been serving with the Free French Forces.[110]

I looked for answers in my father's war journal, but in vain. He had changed his name from Robert Schwartz to Robert Sinclair when he'd enlisted in the army,[111] to protect his parents, who remained in Paris, and to prevent the Germans, who probably had a list of French officers loyal to General de Gaulle, from seeing the connection between him and his family. However, what I did find in his notebooks were writings of his distress at witnessing his own father's death, and his disgust at the "barbarism of the Boches."

In the past, when my father had read to me from his journal, he had not spared me from the details of his mobilization on the Maginot Line in the Ardennes Forest, during the "Phony War"; nor from his tears when describing the German soldiers marching under the Arc de Triomphe down the Champs-Élysées—an image we all know by heart that so poignantly represents France's crushing defeat under the Nazis' boots—nor his determination to join General de Gaulle.

So I knew everything about his long journey to reach Cairo, Damascus, and Beirut, and the years he spent there while the führer's disinformation was spreading throughout the Middle East and he was mainly in charge of countering it with Gaullist messaging. He had rather proudly shown me a dispatch that contained an extract from a speech by Joseph Goebbels, the Reich's minister of propaganda, who in a speech on Radio Beirut had condemned my father, whom he called "the Jew Sinclair," to death.

During all that time, having no way to communicate with his family, my father was unaware of what had happened, and found out only when he returned to Paris just weeks before the German capitulation to the Allies.

Why, then, didn't my father end my confusion when I thought that my grandfather had been imprisoned in Drancy, not in Royallieu-Compiègne? And why didn't he talk to me about my grandfather's months of suffering there? Why didn't he explain how my grandparents had been hunted after the Val-de-Grâce hospitalization and, to avoid being deported, had been forced into hiding? It was as if his living in the present, leaving the past behind, was an imperative for his sanity, and for the well-being of everyone who had experienced the savagery of the Nazis.

One of my deepest curiosities, though, was fed by following my parents' discovery of the insidious role played by the French collaborator Jean Leguay. With northern and western France under occupation, he was the deputy police chief and the representative for another French collaborator, the secretary-general of the Vichy police,

René Bousquet, whose reputation for evil was widely known. Though Jean Leguay was actively involved in the deportation of Jews from France and more, he succeeded in hiding his past for thirty years, before finally being charged for his role in the *rafle du Vél' d'Hiv*. Due to the tenacity of Serge Klarsfeld, he was indicted in 1979 for crimes against humanity. He died ten years later, in 1989, without ever having stood trial.

He and my father had been colleagues in the cosmetics industry, he as CEO of Gemey,[112] my father as CEO of Elizabeth Arden. Both of them also had little country houses in the village of Fleury-en-Bière, in the Seine-et-Marne region, about an hour south of Paris. They saw each other professionally in the city, but they sometimes also met up on weekends in Fleury-en-Bière. I can remember Jean Leguay coming to our house for tea and, as a little girl, sometimes accompanying him and my father on walks near Fontainebleau and its beautiful forest. We had no idea, of course, about his past, which he had skillfully whitewashed in the 1950s to such a degree that he had even been reinstated in the *corps préfectoral*, the regional government, from which he had been expelled at the time of the liberation.

In 1967, when my father discovered Jean Leguay's high-profile role as a Nazi sympathizer, especially in the *rafle du Vél' d'Hiv*, where the higher-ups in the French National Police, in which he was second-in-command, had themselves suggested that children be included in the convoys, he let him know of his disgust.[113] My father let him know, too, that those policemen were also responsible for my grandfather's arrest and internment at Royallieu-Compiègne. Because in the *rafle* of prominent Jews on December 12, 1941, we know that while the Germans had organized the raid, the French police played a key role.[114]

How is it that my father knew so few of the details of his own father's story that he could be fooled? Papa's uncertainty about the misfortunes of our family continued with my own lack of appetite to know more about what had actually happened. It was as if the lack of curiosity about that period had been transmitted from father to daughter. Of course, it was understandable that people wanted to turn the page on the war. But when I became an adult, why didn't I try to understand this tragic, fatal period in my grandfather's life? This was inexplicable to me, especially since I usually want to learn about everything. And so, because I was very late in starting, I never found the answers to the questions I hadn't asked and that still haunt me today. Too late.

This is surely the reason why I immersed myself in the stories of the prisoners themselves, delved into the research carried out by historians. And searched out narratives like the one by Philippe Bernard, the journalist at *Le Monde*, the nephew of Louis Engelmann, my grandfather's neighbor at the Rue de Tocqueville, in which he describes how his uncle told of his wife, Mariette's, incredible bravery.[115] Armed with a letter from the French lawyer Fernand de Brinon[116] addressed to her husband's' employer, Tréfileries et Laminoirs du Havre, she miraculously succeeded in preventing him from being deported to a death camp; instead he was sent to Drancy, and she managed to get him out of there, too. Once again, we see the failings of a system that believed it was perfect.

I have not found all the light I sought on my grandfather's arrest, imprisonment, and liberation. I did not, therefore, manage to bring to life the family saga I had imagined I would. In undertaking to write this book, I'd also hoped to fill the void of lost memories. I went in search of a story and found hundreds of others, many far more tragic than my own family's.

At Royallieu-Compiègne today, the names of many of the prisoners, whether released or deported, are engraved on glass tablets at the entrance to the memorial museum. But my grandfather's was not; he was missing from the glass in the same way he had been missing from my memory. I submitted a request to the museum that the name of Léonce Schwartz be engraved beside those of all the men who had passed through this place; that request was granted in the summer of 2020, and it is for me, along with this book, a gesture I could still make to create more of a bond between us.

As such, my grandfather remains a soul who passes through this story. But the effort to find some trace of him from those months in 1941 and 1942 at Royallieu-Compiègne has also allowed me to bring awareness to a harrowing and little-known tragedy in history and has given me the determination to pass this story on to my children and grandchildren.

When I finished my research, all that was left for me to do was to write the pages you have just read. I have tried to give a bit of dignity and, in a very fleeting way, a new breath of life to those men taken in the *rafle* of prominent Jews, and held at the "camp of slow death," to all those deported, to all those who survived, and to the many more who were so tragically murdered.

ACKNOWLEDGMENTS

First, I want to bow before the memory of those who were interned at Royallieu-Compiègne, both the deported and the survivors. Without their determination to bear witness, this story would not be known to us, and this book would not exist. It is, in fact, largely based on their testimonies, the little there is to be found—but so definitive that I felt bound to quote from them as I went along.

I thank Serge Klarsfeld with all my heart for the friendly kindness he showed toward this project, and for the body of work he has published. His books and essays have nourished my meager knowledge about the *rafle* of those prominent men and of Frontstalag 122.

All my thanks to Laurent Joly, who, with his wealth of knowledge about the period, was kind enough to supply the historical details I needed.

NOTES

1. The original poem as engraved on the monument in Paris. — *Translator:*

   J'ai reve tellement fort
   De toi—j'ai tellement
   Marche tellement parle
   Tellement aime ton ombre
   Qu'il ne me reste plus
   Rien de toi—il me reste
   D'etre l'ombre entre les
   Ombres l'ombre qui viendra
   Et reviendra dans ta vie
   Ensoleillee   R Desnos

   This epigraph is an addition to the English-language edition and is not included in the book's original publication in French. Please see note 34.—*Publisher*

2. More details on the events surrounding my maternal grandparents, the Rosenbergs, can be found in my book *21, rue La Boétie* (Paris: Grasset, 2012); published in English as *My Grandfather's Gallery: A Family Memoir of Art and War* (New York: Farrar, Straus and Giroux, 2014).

3. Drancy, opened in August 1941 in the northeastern part of Paris, was a major internment and transit camp for the deportation of Jews from France.—*Publisher*

4. The term *rafle* is inextricably linked to the arrest, deportation, and subsequent murder of French Jews during World War II. Though sometimes accommodated in translation as "roundup," I have retained the word throughout the text as there is no equivalent in English with such a powerful connotation.—*Translator*

5. One of the historians who attempted to understand its importance is Laurent Joly. See, in particular, his books *Vichy dans la "solution finale," 1941–1944* [Vichy and the "Final Solution," 1941–1944] (Paris: Grasset, 2006) and *L'Etat contre les Juifs* [The State Against the Jews] (Paris: Grasset, 2018).

6. Quoted by Laurent Joly in *L'Etat contre les Juifs*. Joly cites as a reference Raul Hilberg, the author of *La Destruction des Juifs d'Europe* (published in English as *The Destruction of the European Jews*).

7. Auschwitz, also known as Auschwitz-Birkenau, is the German name for the city of Oświęcim in Poland. —*Publisher*

8. Aryanization refers to the forced forfeiture of Jewish-run businesses through massive theft of private property under the authority of Adolf Hitler's would-be successor, Hermann Göring, *Reichsmarschall des Grossdeutschen Reiches,* marshal of the greater German empire.—*Publisher*

9. During World War II, the Free Zone, the Zone Libre, was a territory in the south of France administered by the Vichy government, which, despite the zone's name, was still sympathetic to the Nazis. The rest of the country was occupied by Germany and administrated under its authority; it was known as the Zone Occupée (the Occupied Zone).—*Publisher*

10. Tristan Bernard was a novelist and playwright, particularly known for his witticisms.

11. The playwright Jean-Jacques Bernard, arrested in the *rafle* on December 12, 1941, had the good fortune of being liberated. His book was among the first to be published after the liberation: *Le Camp de la mort lente: Compiègne 1941–1942* (Paris: Albin Michel, 1944; translated into English as *The Camp of Slow Death*). It was republished in the series *Témoignages de la Shoah* [*Witness Statements from the Shoah*].

12. See my book *21, rue La Boétie.*

13. Named after Baron Georges Eugene Haussmann, this was a period beginning in 1853 during which vast renovations of Paris were undertaken to modernize the city. —*Publisher*

14. A division of the French equivalent of the United States Postal Service.—*Translator*

15. The Feldgendarmerie was a military organization within the Third Reich with far-reaching policing authority.—*Publisher*

16. Louis and Mariette Engelmann, *Sans toi, je serais en route pour un grand voyage, histoire d'un sauvetage, Compiègne-Drancy, 1941–1942* [Without You, I Would Be Headed for a Long Journey: The Story of a Rescue, Compiègne-Drancy, 1941–1942], in the series *Témoignages de la Shoah*.

17. The German police and Security Service of the SS, all under the orders of Reinhard Heydrich, SS-Reichsführer Heinrich Himmler's second-in-command. —*Publisher*

18. Saül Castro et al., *Le Camp juif de Royallieu-Compiègne, 1941–1943*, in the series *Témoignages de la Shoah* (Paris: Éditions Le Manuscrit, 2007).

19. Ibid.

20. Commemorative Plaque to the Deported Men place de l'École Militaire, Paris, 7th arrondissment

On December 12, 1941,

The German military police, assisted by the French police,
arrested 743 Important Jewish Frenchmen,
the majority were former combatants
and professional people, and took them to the riding arena
of "Commandant Bossut" at the École Militaire.

The 743 men were interned in the German
camp at Royallieu at Compiegne, where some
died of hunger and the cold.

On March 27, 1942, most of the 743 were deported
on the first convoy that left France for Auschwitz,
where they were killed.

May we never forget those victims of racial hatred.

*The Sons and Daughters of Jewish Deportees from France
Josette and Jean-Jacques FRAENKEL in memory of their Father*

—*Publisher*

21. Theodor Dannecker was a representative of Adolf
    Eichmann, the top man in the Gestapo in charge of the
    "Jewish Question" in France until August 1942. After
    holding this position in France, Dannecker became the
    head of Jewish Affairs in Bulgaria, part of Eichmann's
    team in Hungary, and ended his career by deporting
    Jews from Italy. Captured at the end of the war, he
    hanged himself in an American prison in 1945.
    —*Publisher*

22. A *Militärbefehlshaber* was a military governor, part of
    the German military command in France.—*Publisher*

23. Quoted in Roger Gompel, "Pour que tu n'oublies pas"
    [So You Don't Forget], in Castro et al., *Le Camp juif de
    Royallieu-Compiègne.*

24. Georges Wellers was arrested on December 12, 1941;
    transferred to Drancy on April 3, 1942; and deported to
    Auschwitz on June 30, 1944. After his release and until
    his death in 1991, he dedicated his life to the history of
    the Shoah and the struggle against Holocaust
    denialism.

25. Otto Abetz, the German ambassador to France, con-
    firmed that this *rafle* was organized as a reprisal. In a
    note sent on December 7 to the German minister of
    foreign affairs, cited by Georges Wellers, Abetz explic-
    itly said this: "Even though it has been clearly proven

that the perpetrators [of the attacks] are Frenchmen, it is better not to emphasize that fact, but rather to take into account our political interests and claim that it was exclusively the actions of Jews and spies in the pay of the Anglo-Saxon and Soviet secret services." Nothing could be clearer.

26. Michael Marrus and Robert Paxton, *Vichy et les Juifs*, 2nd ed. (Paris: Calmann-Lévy, 2015).

27. The number 743 is known by all the period specialists, but the list itself, the one called "The 743," has disappeared. Serge Klarsfeld provided me with 87 names found at the Sons and Daughters of Jewish Deportees from France (FFDJF). This was the first attempt made after the war to identify the "influential" Jews who were arrested. May this book and the ongoing research allow us to complete that gruesome list as much as possible.

28. The French Revolution made Jews full citizens, liberating them. —*Publisher*

29. Claude Weill, "Le dernier Juif de Westhoffen," *Le Nouvel Observateur*, October 28, 1999.

30. *Gros* can be translated as "fat," "large," or "big." —*Translator*

31. Literal translation: Royal Place. —*Translator*

32. Royallieu was used as a military camp after the First World War. In 1939 and 1940, the French converted some barracks into a military hospital during the Phony War. In June 1940, the occupying German

forces reconfigured the camp into Frontstalag 122 to hold military prisoners. In December 1941, they began holding civilian prisoners there, too; that is when this story takes place.—*Publisher*

33. "Phony War" refers to the period beginning in September 1939 when France and the United Kingdom had declared war against Germany but for eight months no major military action occurred.—*Translator*

34. Robert Desnos was deported from France in April 1944 and died on June 8, 1945, at the Theresienstadt concentration camp in Czechoslovakia.—*Publisher*

35. The majority of the seventy-six thousand French Jews deported between 1941 and 1944 were first held in Drancy; only two thousand of them returned.

36. The "American Camp" was established when the United States entered the war. At that time, Americans living in France were arrested and imprisoned at Royallieu-Compiègne.—*Publisher*

37. "White Russians" refers to Russian anti-Communist political prisoners, "Red Russians" to Russian Communists captured in battle.—*Publisher*

38. "Twice a day, at eight in the morning and at six in the evening, the inmates lined up in front of the blocks (buildings) in columns of five. In 1941 and early 1942, roll calls were held in all camps at the same time. The call started with the American Camp, then the Russian Camp, the French Camp (political) and it ended with the Jewish Camp (Camp C), so that the Jewish

internees remained outside, in any weather (the cold, the rain) half an hour to three-quarters of an hour . . . although . . . sometimes for several consecutive hours. The long roll calls were due to the stupidity of the German noncommissioned officers, they did not know how to count without making a mistake," wrote Adam Rutkowski in Castro et al., *Le Camp juif de Royallieu-Compiègne.—Publisher*

39. Sonderführer Kuntze's first name cannot be verified. The same is true for Major Furtwängler, the head German medical officer at Frontstalag 122. Once the Germans saw the beginning of their defeat, they destroyed all official registers that could be used as evidence against them.—*Publisher*

40. On December 14, 1941.—*Publisher*

41. Boldo was short for Boldoflorine, a famous herbal drink, created in 1933, said to be good for the liver.

42. The second mass arrest of Jews took place between August 20 and August 23, 1941, in retaliation for anti-Occupation acts. It was "suggested by Dannecker who was carrying out his program of creation of special camps in the occupied zone, and of filling them with Jews. The Parisian municipal police was responsible for the implementation of this measure, with the assistance of Feldgendames" (Serge Klarsfeld, *Vichy-Auschwitz: Le Rôle de Vichy dans la question juive en France* [Paris: Fayard, 1983]). More than forty-two hundred Jews (men, including fifteen hundred Frenchmen) were arrested and taken to the new

Drancy camp (Renée Poznanski, *Être juif en France pendant la Seconde Guerre mondiale* [Paris: Hachette, 1994]).—*Publisher*

43. The future Nobel laureate in literature André Gide, the great French lyric poet François Villon, and the nineteenth-century French poet Gérard de Nerval. —*Publisher*

44. François Montel and Georges Kohn, *Journal de Compiègne et de Drancy* (Paris: Éditions FFDJF, 1999).

45. Benjamin Schatzman, *Journal d'un interné, Compiègne, Drancy, Pithiviers, 12 décembre 1941–23 septembre 1942*, vols. 1 and 2, in the series *Témoignages de la Shoah* [*Witness Statements of the Shoah*] (Paris: Éditions Le Manuscrit, 2005). Rereleased in 2006 by Fayard. The original document is located at the Mémorial de la Shoah, a Holocaust museum in Paris.

46. Jean-Jacques Bernard, *Le Camp de la mort lente.*

47. The prisoners' gradual degradation helps explain why they came to call it "Le Camp de la mort lente," "The Camp of Slow Death."—*Publisher*

48. Interview with Serge Klarsfeld, August 2019.

49. François Darlan was the head of the Vichy government from February 1941 until Pierre Laval returned in April 1942.

50. Joly, *L'État contre les Juifs.*

51. Ibid.

52. Xavier Vallat was replaced in 1942 by Louis Darquier de Pellepoix, an anti-Semite more submissive to the Germans.—*Publisher*

53. See page 36 regarding the release of elderly or sick men on December 20.

54. Marrus and Paxton, *Vichy et les Juifs.*

55. The Vichy government believed that the French people would be more accepting of state-sponsored persecution of foreign Jews than of nationals. —*Publisher*

56. Vichy initially intended to prioritize persecuting foreign Jews over French Jewish citizens, though later the distinction was dropped and the government persecuted both.—*Publisher*

57. This notion of "kind soldiers of the regular army" is an extension of the "myth of the clean Wehrmacht," which has been dispelled unequivocally. It falsely claims that the Nazi unified armed forces, the Wehrmacht, played no part in the Holocaust. —*Publisher*

58. Roger Gompel in Castro et al., *Le Camp juif de Royallieu-Compiègne.*

59. Henri Jacob-Rick and Georges Wellers in Castro et al., *Le Camp juif de Royallieu-Compiègne.*

60. The Hebrew word *aliyah* means "ascension" and is used to designate a Jew's emigration to the land of Israel.

61. Schatzman, *Journal d'un interné.*

62. The original journal of Henri Jacob-Rick is also at the Mémorial de la Shoah.

63. Saül Castro in Castro et al., *Le Camp juif de Royallieu-Compiègne.*

64. Georges Wellers in Castro et al., *Le Camp juif de Royallieu-Compiègne.* See also the notes by Serge Klarsfeld in Montel and Kohn, *Journal de Compiègne et de Drancy.*

65. Pierre Masse was an esteemed lawyer, a member of the Council of the Order, a former minister under Prime Minister Paul Painlevé, and then a senator in the French parliament. After France fell to the Germans, he protested against Vichy's requirement in February 1941 that all parliament members announce any Jewish ancestry. He was arrested on August 21, and held at Drancy and Royallieu-Compiègne. Maréchal Pétain sent a request to the German authorities for Senator Masse's release from a French prison in Paris, but it was denied. On September 30, 1942, he was deported to Auschwitz, where he died the following month.—*Publisher*

66. Pierre and Roger Masse would be deported to Auschwitz and would perish there within months of each other: Roger on July 27, 1942, at age fifty-seven; Pierre a few months later, in October, at age sixty-two.—*Publisher*

67. See Robert Badinter, "Mort d'un Israélite français: Hommage à maître Pierre Masse" [Death of a French Jew], *Le Débat* 158, no. 1 (January–February 2010): 101–107.

68. Ibid.

69. No notations were found for my grandfather except for the reference in Jean-Jacques Engelmann's narrative upon his arrest and transfer to the town hall of the Seventeenth Arrondissement, as detailed in chapter 1.

70. Jean-Jacques Bernard, *Le Camp de la mort lente.*

71. The Third Republic was the term used for the French government from 1870 to 1940. It provided a generally stable environment for social advancements and economic growth and ended with the fall of France to the Germans, when it was succeeded by the Nazi-sympathizing Vichy government. —*Publisher*

72. From the journal of Henri Jacob-Rick at the Mémorial de la Shoah.

73. Georges Wellers in Castro et al., *Le Camp juif de Royallieu-Compiègne.* —*Publisher*

74. Robert Netter was born on November 21, 1913, in Paris. He was deported on March 27, 1942, in the first convoy that left Royallieu-Compiègne for Auschwitz, where he was killed on April 27, at the age of twenty-eight. —*Publisher*

75. Adam Rutkowski in Castro et al., *Le Camp juif de Royallieu-Compiègne.*

76. Abraham Alpérine was a leader of Amelot, the Parisian underground Jewish rescue organization formed in June 1940, and Georges Cogniot was a member of the

Central Committee of the French Communist Party.
—*Publisher*

77. The rumor that Kiev had been retaken was false. But it sparked hope that the war would end quickly. In fact, it would be two years before Ukraine was taken back by the Russians, on or around Christmas Eve 1943.—*Publisher*

78. The Nazis' first operational center for mass murder opened on December 8, 1941, in Chelmno, Poland. The inefficient method initially used there, of gassing Jews by funneling a truck's carbon monoxide–laden exhaust fumes into a closed room, was a precursor to the Nazis' machinery that would ultimately exterminate six million Jewish lives.—*Publisher*

79. Alphonse Allais was a writer and humorist, Tristan Bernard a playwright, and Georges Courteline a novelist.—*Publisher*

80. "Georges Wellers bore witness in an unforgettable manner" during the trial of Adolf Eichmann in Jerusalem in 1961, according to Serge Klarsfeld in his notes in Montel and Kohn's *Journal de Compiègne et de Drancy*. Wellers did so again during the trial of Kurt Lischka in Cologne in 1979, "recalling the martyrdom of thousands of Jewish children in France, deported right before his eyes in August of 1942." Lischka was the Nazi chief of police, *Kommandant* of the Sipo-SD of Paris (the police and Security Service of the SS). In 1971, he was discovered living in Cologne, West Germany, by Serge Klarsfeld and his wife, Beate.

81. Adam Rutkowski in Castro et al., *Le Camp juif de Royallieu-Compiègne.*

82. These influential French Jews were among a very integrated and privileged population whose ancestry in France could be traced for centuries. In the nineteenth century and the beginning of the twentieth, they called themselves *Israélites,* mostly to distinguish themselves in a patronizing way from foreign Jews living in France who had emigrated from central and eastern Europe more recently.—*Publisher*

83. The ancien régime refers to the period in French history from the Late Middle Ages until the French Revolution. Here the turn of phrase is used to indicate that in the ancien régime, Jews did not have citizenship status but became full citizens as a result of the French Revolution.—*Translator*

84. *Mein Kampf* was published without authorization by the French publishing house Nouvelles Éditions Latines, founded by the anti-Semite and fascist sympathizer Fernand Sorlot. Adolf Hitler subsequently sued the publisher on June 18, 1934; was awarded a cash settlement of 80,000 francs; and allowed the publisher to continue selling the book. By the start of the war in 1939, it had already been translated into eleven languages worldwide.—*Publisher*

85. "Boches" was a derogatory term to describe Germans that was in common usage among those who lived through the war.—*Publisher*

86. See Serge Klarsfeld's preface to Louis and Mariette Engelmann's *Sans toi, je serais en route pour un grand voyage*.

87. Jean-Jacques Bernard, *Le Camp de la mort lente*.

88. Roger Gompel in Castro et al., *Le Camp juif de Royallieu-Compiègne*.

89. The men themselves alternated between using these two adjectives, "cold-blooded" and "chilling."

90. *Rafle du Vél' d'Hiv* is an abbreviation for *Rafle du Vélodrome d'Hiver*, the mass arrest of Jews in Paris by the French police on July 16 and 17, 1942. Some thirteen thousand men, women, and children were arrested; sent temporarily to a sports stadium, the *Vélodrome d'Hiver*; and then deported, mainly to Auschwitz. — *Translator*

91. Saül Castro in Castro et al., *Le Camp juif de Royallieu-Compiègne*.

92. Reinhard Heydrich, who played a major role in the extermination of Jews, both before and after that meeting, was SS-Reichsführer Heinrich Himmler's trusted ally, whom Adolf Hitler described, according to the biographer Mario Dederichs, as "the man with the iron heart," and whom his victims called "Hangman Heydrich" and "the Butcher of Prague." — *Publisher*

93. Laurent Joly in *L'Etat contre les Juifs*.

94. Georges Wellers in Castro et al., *Le Camp juif de Royallieu-Compiègne*.

95. Records at the Holocaust memorial museum in Royallieu-Compiègne indicate that Mr. Rabinovitch's first name could be Théodore, but that cannot be proven as of yet.—*Publisher*

96. From Solange de Lalène's 1980 introduction to the publication of her father's testimony in Castro et al., *Le Camp juif de Royallieu-Compiègne.*

97. The insertion of this quotation within the body of the book is an addition to the English-language edition and is not included in the book's original publication in French.—*Publisher*

98. After the men from the December 12, 1941, *rafle* were removed from the camp, it was again used to hold prisoners, both Jewish and not, until the end of the German occupation on August 25, 1944.—*Publisher*

99. Telegram No. WUE 20829, cited by Georges Wellers in Castro et al., *Le Camp juif de Royallieu-Compiègne.*

100. Ibid.

101. Ibid.

102. The original documents of the "negotiations" between Berlin and Dannecker are at the Mémorial de la Shoah, in Paris.

103. Adam Rutkowski in Castro et al., *Le Camp juif de Royallieu-Compiègne.*

104. After January 20, 1942, the date of the Wannsee Conference.

105. Badinter, "Mort d'un Israélite français: Hommage à maître Pierre Masse."

106. Frontstalag 122 prisoners were transferred to the hospital when they were about to die. But very often, German officials would come to check on how they were doing; and if they were feeling better, they would be sent back to the camp to be deported.—*Publisher*

107. Shortly after this book was originally published in France in March 2020, the niece of the portraitist contacted Ms. Sinclair to inform her that the gentleman's name was Marcel Lhermann. He was a very good designer and painter. Tragically, he was taken from the hospital, sent back to Compiègne, and deported to Auschwitz, where he was killed in a gas chamber at age thirty-seven.—*Publisher*

108. More commonly known as the "yellow star," because it was made of yellow fabric cut in the shape of a Star of David; in its center was the French word *Juif,* "Jew." —*Publisher*

109. The German High Command unconditionally surrendered all its forces to General Dwight D. Eisenhower at Reims, in northeastern France, on May 7, 1945. —*Publisher*

110. The Free French Forces, the "Gaullists," were French Resistance fighters under General Charles de Gaulle, who would later serve as president of France (1958–1969).—*Publisher*

III. Ms. Sinclair's father had tried to join de Gaulle's Free France in England, but could not find a way to travel there. Instead he went to the United States, where he was able to enlist in the Free French Forces and accept an assignment.—*Publisher*

112. Gemey was bought in 1973 by the L'Oréal group, where certain collaborators ended up after the war, but that's another story . . .

113. In fact, there were arrests of 12,884 Jews, including 4,051 children.—*Publisher*

114. From Ms. Sinclair's earlier book, *My Grandfather's Gallery*: "My father, that day in 1967, had difficulty believing that the official who had taken an active role in those deportation-related activities was the same Leguay with whom, the previous weekend, he had shared a friendly cup of tea."—*Publisher*

115. From Engelmann and Engelmann, *Sans toi, je serais en route pour un grand voyage*. The story tells of Louis's "extraordinary rescue" by his wife, Mariette, from the platform of the train station at Compiègne on March 27, 1942, from which a convoy of deportees to Auschwitz was leaving. Their nephew Philippe Bernard, a journalist at *Le Monde*, who later took on the task of organizing, then publishing their two intertwining journals, wrote the introduction to the book.

116. Fernand de Brinon was also a representative of the Vichy government in the Occupied Zone—in a way, Vichy's "ambassador" to the Germans.

BIBLIOGRAPHY

Badinter, Robert. "Mort d'un Israélite français: Hommage à maître Pierre Masse" [Death of a French Jew]. *Le Débat* 158, no. 1 (January–February 2010).

Bernard, Jean-Jacques. *Le Camp de la mort lente: Compiègne, 1941–1942*. Paris: Albin Michel, 1944. Reprinted in the *Témoignages de la Shoah* series. Paris: Éditions Le Manuscrit, 2006.

Castro, Saül, Roger Gompel, Henri Jacob-Rick, Georges Kohn, Robert-Lazare Rousso, Adam Rutkowski, and Georges Wellers. *Le Camp juif de Royallieu-Compiègne, 1941–1943*. *Témoignages de la Shoah* series. Paris: Éditions Le Manuscrit, 2007.

Engelmann, Louis, and Mariette Engelmann. *Sans toi, je serais en route pour un grand voyage: Histoire d'un sauvetage, Compiègne-Drancy, 1941–1942* [Without You, I Would Be Headed for a Long Journey: The Story of a Rescue, Compiègne-Drancy, 1941–1942]. *Témoignages de la Shoah* series. Paris: Éditions Le Manuscrit, 2016.

Joly, Laurent. *L'État contre les Juifs* [The State Against the Jews]. Paris: Grasset, 2018.

———. *Vichy dans la "solution finale," 1941–1944* [Vichy and the "Final Solution," 1941–1944]. Paris: Grasset, 2006.

Klarsfeld, Beate, and Serge Klarsfeld. *Le Mémorial de la Déportation des Juifs de France* [*The Memorial to the Deportation of the Jews of France*]. Paris: Fayard, 1978; reedited in the *La Shoah en France* collection, 4 vols. Paris: Fayard, 2001.

Klarsfeld, Serge. *Vichy-Auschwitz, Le Rôle de Vichy dans la question juive en France* [*Vichy-Auschwitz, The Role of Vichy in the Jewish Question in France*], 2 vols. Paris: Fayard, 1983; reedited in the *La Shoah en France* collection, vol. 1. Paris: Fayard, 2018.

———. *Le Calendrier de la persécution des Juifs de France, 1940–1944* [*The Calendar of the Persecution of the Jews of France, 1940-1944*]. New York: Les Fils et Filles des déportés juifs de France [The Sons and Daughters of Jewish Deportees from France], Beate Klarsfeld Foundation, 1993.

Marrus, Michael R., and Robert O. Paxton. *Vichy et les Juifs*. 2nd ed. Paris: Édition Calmann-Lévy, 2015. Published in English as *Vichy France and the Jews.* New York: Basic Books, 1981.

Montel, François, and Georges Kohn. *Journal de Compiègne et de Drancy*. With an introduction and annotations by Serge Klarsfeld. Paris: Éditions FFDJF, 1999.

Poznanski, Renée. *Être juif en France pendant la Seconde Guerre mondiale*. Paris: Hachette, 1994. Published in English as *Jews in France During World War II*. Hanover, NH: University Press of New England for Brandeis University Press in association with the United States Holocaust Memorial Museum, 2001.

Schatzman, Benjamin. *Journal d'un interné: Compiègne, Drancy, Pithiviers, 12 décembre 1941–23 septembre 1942*. 2 vols. *Témoignages de la Shoah* series. Paris: Éditions Le Manuscrit, 2005. Reprinted in 2006 by Fayard.

Scheid, Élie. *Histoire des Juifs d'Alsace*. Cressé, France: Éditions des Régionalismes, 2017.

Sinclair, Anne. *21, rue La Boétie*. Paris: Grasset, 2012.

Weill, Claude. "Le dernier Juif de Westhoffen." *Le Nouvel Observateur*, no. 1825 (October 28, 1999).